LES NOUVELLES FRANCES

The publication of this work was assisted by
major grants from the
Florence J. Gould Foundation
and
The Rhode Island Committee for the Humanities.

1. Le Chasteau. 2. Le Jardin. 3. La Basse cour. 4. La Chapelle et les Offices. 5. Les Escuries. 6. La Tour des munitions. 7. La Ville d'Angole.

Les Nouvelles Frances
France in America, 1500–1815
An Imperial Perspective

by Philip P. Boucher
The University of Alabama in Huntsville

The John Carter Brown Library
Providence, Rhode Island
1989

FRONTISPIECE:
"Isle de S. Christophe" from
Charles de Rochefort, *Histoire
naturelle et morale des îles Antilles
de l'Amérique* (1665).
The much vaunted plantation
estate of Governor Poincy,
who for two decades (1640–
60) was the autonomous
ruler of the French colony at
St. Christopher. On the right
is the slave village, the "town
of Angola."

The John Carter Brown Library is an independently funded and administered center
for advanced research in the humanities at
Brown University.

This exhibition catalogue was published on
the occasion of the opening of the Library's
exhibition, "Les Nouvelles Frances," in the
spring of 1989. The exhibition was mounted
to commemorate the bicentennial of the outbreak of the French Revolution.

ISBN 0-916617-32-7

Special thanks to my mother,
Loretta Poulin Boucher,
for her support and understanding.

CONTENTS

ILLUSTRATIONS

Foreword

FEW EVENTS in all of human history have had such far-reaching repercussions as the French Revolution. To venture to list even some of these is to invite criticism for leaving others out. Without the French Revolution, for example, Karl Marx could never have developed a theory of world Communist revolution, with its enormous impact on the twentieth century. Without the French Revolution, the formation and character of the modern nation-state, including the unification of Germany and Italy in the nineteenth century, would not have taken the shape it did. No event did more for the establishment in international law of the concept of individual human rights than the French Revolution, to which all of the world is heir.

The controversy swirling around the French Revolution at the time of its occurrence entered directly into the political dialogue in the new United States in the 1790s, with subtle consequences for the development of American politics. But perhaps even more important, the black revolution for independence in Haiti, which was a direct consequence of the French Revolution and resulted in the creation of the second republic in the New World, sent shock waves through slave-holding societies everywhere in the Western Hemisphere, not least the southern United States. The result was a fateful hardening of positions on the issues posed by the terrible heritage of two centuries of the importation of African slave labor into colonial British America. Finally, it was the loss of Haiti (or Saint Domingue) by the French that convinced Napoleon he should sell the Louisiana territory, thereby doubling the size of the United States.

This year, 1989, the bicentennial of its outbreak, will see numerous programs and events dedicated to commemorating the French Revolution. A few years back, when members of the staff of the John Carter Brown Library first began to think about an appropriate project that this institution might contribute to the anniversary celebration, it was decided that the Library should play to its strength, namely its nearly unrivaled holdings of printed materials relating to French exploration and colonization in the Americas. In particular, the Library could offer a comprehensive view of these French endeavors over a 250-year period, incorporating areas normally ignored or forgotten when French enterprise in America is mentioned. French ships and soldiers and merchants and priests were committed not only to exploration and colonization in Canada, the Mississippi basin, and the Caribbean, but also, for a time, in Brazil, Guiana, and "Florida" (meaning the region extending from present-day Florida through South Carolina). The story is one of epic scope, beginning with the French-sponsored first voyage of Verrazzano and ending with the final defeat of Napoleon.

It was a happy circumstance that a long-time friend of the Library, Professor Philip Boucher of the University of Alabama in Huntsville, was available to write the text for an exhibition on the scale described above. A specialist in French colonial history who had earned his Ph.D. at the nearby University of Connecticut and who had also been a research Fellow at the JCB, Professor Boucher knew the Library's collection well and was highly qualified for the task. At the very beginning of the project, Professor Boucher and the Library staff agreed that we would try to produce a work that offered more than was typical of the genre of exhibition catalogues. Professor Boucher was encouraged to write a succinct narrative survey of French colonial activities in the Americas in the first three hundred years (a work much-needed in general), using as primary sources the Library's extraordinary collection of French books from the period.

The result, as the reader will see, is an unusual and eminently successful volume that accomplishes many of the purposes of a standard exhibition catalogue but goes beyond the typical example. We have here a true work of history into which is quietly integrated over 130 citations to primary sources found in the John Carter Brown Library collection.

In order to make the book function as an exhibition catalogue we have supplied at the beginning a complete list of the primary sources in order of appearance, each given a bracketed number. These bracketed numbers are used throughout the text as reference keys to the sources. At the end of the volume, there is an alphabetical author-title list of all of these primary sources, which provides another access point to the works.

The achievement represented by the text of this volume is Professor Boucher's entirely. However, as always in the making of a book, help is garnered from many directions. Professor Boucher in his introduction has mentioned some of the people from whom he received assistance. It is my pleasant duty here to acknowledge some others. Susan Newbury, Chief of Cataloguing at the Library, took responsibility for the accuracy of the bibliographical apparatus, preparing both the list of primary sources cited and the alphabetical index to the list. As anyone with experience in the field of rare books knows, the proper citation and attribution of author, title, and date and place of publication must often be "established," since many of the references in the existing literature may be incorrect in form or content. Sonia Galletti, a much-valued Library volunteer, organized the illustrations for the volume. As is usual for JCBL publications, the shooting of the illustrations was wholly accomplished by the Library's staff photographer, Richard E. Hurley. Finally, copy-editing and indexing of the volume was performed by Eta Fox Wayne, under the auspices of Editorial Services of New England, in Cambridge, Massachusetts.

The publication of this catalogue is part of a larger French Revolution Bicentennial project at the John Carter Brown Library, which also includes a symposium on French and American relations from the seventeenth century to the twentieth and a lecture series on the French heritage in New England.

It is a pleasure to recognize here the grant support of the L.J. Skaggs and Mary C. Skaggs Foundation for this project, a timely personal contribution from Robert S. Pirie, and the financial assistance of the Québec Delegation in New England. For support of the research, writing, and editing of this catalogue in particular, the Library wishes to acknowledge with gratitude the generous funding received from the Rhode Island Committee for the Humanities and the encouragement of its Executive Director, Thomas H. Roberts. The Florence J. Gould Foundation generously underwrote the major part of the production costs of the catalogue.

It has been the mission of the John Carter Brown Library for more than 125 years to collect and preserve the documents from the past that help to illuminate the early history of the Americas, and to promote research, publication, and teaching concerning that history. It is our hope that *Les Nouvelles Frances* effectively contributes to the fulfillment of these purposes.

NORMAN FIERING
Director and Librarian

LIST OF PRIMARY SOURCES CITED

[1] Hernán Cortés (1485 – 1547). *Des marches, îles et pays trouvés*. Antwerp, [1522].*

[2] Pietro Martire d'Anghiera (1457 – 1526). *Extraict ou recueil des isles nouvellement trouvées*. Paris, 1532.

[3] *Le Nouveau Monde et navigacions faites par Emeric de Vespuce*. Paris, 1516 (compiled by Fracanzano da Montaboddo; translated by Mathurin du Redouer; sometimes attributed to Amerigo Vespucci).

[4] Gonzalo Fernández de Oviedo y Valdés (1478 – 1557). *L'histoire naturelle et géneralle des Indes*. Paris, 1556.

[5] Peter Apian (1495 – 1552). *La cosmographie*. Antwerp, 1544.

[6] Sebastian Münster (1489 – 1552). *La cosmographie universelle*. [Basel], 1568.

[7] Jacques Cartier (1491 – 1557). *Discours du voyage*. Rouen, 1598.

[8] Antonio Pigafetta (ca. 1480/91 – ca. 1534). *Le voyage et navigation*. Paris, [1525] (abridged and translated by Jacques Antoine Fabre).

[9] Jean Ribaut (ca. 1520 – 1565). *The whole & true discoverye of Terra Florida*. London, [1563].*

[10] *Coppie d'une lettre venant de la Floride envoyée à Rouen*. Paris, 1565.

[11] Francisco López de Gómara (1511 – 1564). *Histoire géneralle des Indes Occidentales*. Paris, 1605 (translated by Martin Fumée).

[12] Abraham Ortelius (1527 – 1598). *Théâtre de l'univers*. Antwerp, 1598.

[13] Peeter Heyns (1537 – 1598). *Le miroir du monde*. Antwerp, 1579.

[14] Bartolomé de las Casas (1474 – 1566). *Tyrannies et cruautéz des Espagnols*. Rouen, 1630 (translated by Jacques de Miggrode).

[15] Girolamo Benzoni (b. 1519). *Histoire nouvelle du Nouveau Monde*. [Geneva], 1579 (translated by Urbain Chauveton).

[16] Nicolas Le Challeux (16th cent.). *Discours de l'histoire de la Floride*. Dieppe, 1566.

[17] *Histoire mémorable de la reprinse de l'isle de la Floride*. [Paris], 1568 (sometimes attributed to Dominique de Gourgues).*

[18] André Thevet (1502 – 1590). *La cosmographie universelle*. Paris, 1575.

[19] André Thevet (1502 – 1590). *Les singularitéz de la France antarctique*. Paris, 1558.

[20] Sebastian Münster (1489 – 1552). *La cosmographie universelle de tout le monde*. Paris, 1575 (edited and translated by François de Belleforest).

[21] Jean de Léry (1534 – 1611). *Histoire d'un voyage fait en la terre du Brésil*. [La Rochelle], 1578.

[22] Lancelot Voisin, sieur de La Popelinière (1541 – 1608). *Les trois mondes*. Paris, 1582.

[23] René Goulaine de Laudonnière (16th cent.). *L'histoire notable de la Floride*. Paris, 1586.

[24] José de Acosta (1540 – 1600). *Histoire*

naturelle et morale des Indes. Paris, 1616 (translated by Robert Regnauld Cauxois).

[25] Samuel de Champlain (1567–1635). *Brief discours des choses plus remarquables.* [Manuscript, ca. 1602].

[26] Samuel de Champlain (1567–1635). *Des sauvages, ou, voyage.* Paris, [1603].

[27] Marc Lescarbot. *Histoire de la Nouvelle France.* Paris, 1609.

[28] Jean Mocquet (b. 1575). *Voyages en Afrique, Asie, Indes Orientales, & Occidentales.* Rouen, 1645.

[29] François Pyrard (ca. 1570–1621). *Voyage.* Paris, 1619.

[30] Claude, d'Abbeville (d. 1632). *Histoire de la mission des pères capucins.* Paris, 1614.

[31] Yves, d'Evreux (1570–1630?). *Suitte de l'histoire des choses plus mémorables.* Paris, 1615.*

[32] Pierre Biard (1565–1622). *Relation de la Nouvelle France.* Lyon, 1616.*

[33] Gabriel Sagard. *Histoire du Canada.* Paris, 1636.

[34] Samuel de Champlain (1567–1635). *Les voyages de la Nouvelle France occidentale, dicte Canada.* Paris, 1632.

[35] Gabriel Sagard. *Le grand voyage du pays des hurons.* Paris, 1632.

[36] Chrétien Le Clercq (fl. 1641–1695). *Etablissement de la foy dans la Nouvelle France.* Paris, 1691.

[37] Paul Le Jeune (1592–1664). *Relation de ce qui s'est passé en la Nouvelle France en l'année 1633.* Paris, 1634.

[38] Paul Le Jeune (1592–1664). *Relation de ce qui s'est passé en la Nouvelle France, es années 1640 et 1641.* Paris, 1642 (also attributed to Barthélemy Vimont).

[39] France. *Loix et constitutions des colonies françoises.* Paris, 1784–[1790] (edited by Médéric Louis Elie Moreau de Saint-Méry).

[40] Jean Baptiste Du Tertre (1610–1687). *Histoire générale des isles de S. Christophe.* Paris, 1654.

[41] Jean Baptiste Du Tertre (1610–1687). *Histoire générale des Antilles.* Paris, 1667–1671.

[42] Jacques Bouton (1592–1658). *Relation de l'éstablissement des François depuis l'an 1635.* Paris, 1640.

[43] Pierre Pelleprat (1609–1667). *Relation des missions des PP. de la Compagnie de Jésus.* Paris, 1655.

[44] Paul Boyer (b. 1615?). *Véritable relation de tout ce qui s'est fait et passé.* Paris, 1654.

[45] *Proiet d'une compagnie pour l'Amérique.* [Paris, 1651].

[46] Compagnie de la France équinoxiale. *Mémoire pour servir de brève instruction.* Paris, 1653.

[47] Israel Silvestre (1621–1691). *La descente faite par les François en la terre ferme de l'Amérique.* [Paris, 1653]. [Print]

[48] Jean de Laon, sieur d'Aigremont. *Relation du voyage des François fait au Cap de Nord en Amérique.* Paris, 1654.

[49] Antoine Biet (b. 1620). *Voyage de la France équinoxiale en l'isle de Cayenne.* Paris, 1664.

[50] Blaise François de Pagan, comte de Merveilles (1604–1665). *Relation historique et géographique.* Paris, 1655.

[51] Pacifique, de Provins (1588–ca. 1649). *Briève relation du voyage des isles de l'Amérique.* Paris, 1646.

[52] Maurile de Saint Michel (d. 1669). *Voyage des isles Camercanes.* Le Mans, 1652.

[53] Charles de Rochefort (b. 1605). *Histoire naturelle et morale des îles Antilles de l'Amérique.* Rotterdam, 1658.

[54] Barthélemy Vimont (1594–1667). *Relation de ce qui s'est passé en la Nou-*

velle France en l'année *1642 & 1643*. Paris, 1644.

[55] Paul Ragueneau (1608–1680). *Relation de ce qui s'est passé de plus remarquable*. Paris, 1652.

[56] Jérôme Lallemant (1592–1673). *Relation de ce qui s'est passé de plus remarquable*. Paris, 1661.

[57] Paul Le Jeune (1592–1664). *Relation de ce qui s'est passé de plus remarquable*. Paris, 1662.

[58] Pierre Boucher (1622–1717). *Histoire véritable et naturelle*. Paris, 1664.

[59] Antoine Joseph Le Febvre de La Barre (d. 1688). *Description de la France équinoctiale*. Paris, 1666.

[60] Jean Clodoré (d. 1731). *Relation de ce qui s'est passé dans les isles & terre-ferme de l'Amérique*. Paris, 1671.

[61] *Recueil de divers voyages faits en Afrique et en l'Amérique*. Paris, 1674 (compiled by Henri Justel).

[62] Cristóbal de Acuña (b. 1597). *Relation de la rivière des Amazones*. Paris, 1682 (translated by Marin Le Roy Gomberville).

[63] Jean Baptiste Labat (1663–1738). *Nouveau voyage aux isles de l'Amérique*. Paris, 1722.

[64] Raymond Breton (1609–1679). *Dictionaire caraibe-françois*. Auxerre, 1665.

[65] Alexandre Olivier Exquemelin. *Histoire des avanturiers*. Paris, 1686.

[66] Thomas Gage (1603?–1656). *Nouvelle relation*. Paris, 1676.

[67] France. *Traité de Neutralité*. Bordeaux, 1687.

[68] Claude Dablon (1618–1697). *Relation de ce qui s'est passé de plus remarquable*. Paris, 1672.

[69] *Nouvelle découverte de plusieurs nations dans la Nouvelle France en l'année 1673*

et 1674 (Manuscript map attributed to Louis Joliet).

[70] Melchisédech Thévenot (1620?–1692). *Recueil de voyages*. Paris, 1681.

[71] Louis Armand de Lom d'Arce, baron de Lahontan (1666–1715?). *Nouveaux voyages*. The Hague, 1703.

[72] Louis Hennepin (ca. 1640–ca. 1705). *Description de la Louisiane*. Paris, 1683.

[73] Henri Joutel (1640?-1735). *Journal historique du dernier voyage que feu M. de la Sale fit*. Paris, 1713.

[74] Louis Hennepin (ca. 1640–ca. 1705). *Nouveau voyage d'un pais plus grand que l'Europe*. Utrecht, 1698.

[75] *Dernières découvertes dans l'Amérique septentrionale*. Paris, 1697 (attributed to Henri de Tonti).

[76] Pierre-François-Xavier de Charlevoix (1682–1761). *Histoire et description générale de la Nouvelle France*. Paris, 1744.

[77] *Voyage de Marseille à Lima*. Paris, 1720 (attributed to Durret).

[78] François Froger (b. 1676). *Relation d'un voyage de la Mer du Sud*. Amsterdam, 1715.

[79] Jean-Bernard-Louis Desjean, baron de Pointis (1645–1707). *Relation de l'expédition de Carthagène*. Amsterdam, 1698.

[80] *Voyages aux côtes de Guinée & en Amérique*. Amsterdam, 1719 (attributed to Monsieur N***).

[81] Gautier du Tronchoy. *Journal de la campagne des isles de l'Amérique*. Troyes, 1709.

[82] Antonio de Solís (1610–1686). *Histoire de la conquête du Mexique*. Paris, 1691 (translated by S. de Broë).

[83] *Relation de ce qui s'est passé en Canada*. [La Rochelle, 1691].

[84] Claude Le Beau. *Avantures*. Amsterdam, 1738.

[85] Claude-Charles Le Roy Bacqueville de La Potherie (1663–1736). *Histoire de l'Amérique septentrionale.* Paris, 1722.

[86] Jean Baptiste Labat (1663 – 1738). *Voyage du chevalier des Marchais en Guinée…et à Cayenne.* Amsterdam, 1731.

[87] Charles Plumier (1646 – 1704). *Description des plantes de l'Amérique.* Paris, 1693.

[88] Charles-Marie de La Condamine (1701 – 1774). *Relation abrégée d'un voyage.* Paris, 1745.

[89] Pierre Barrère (1690–1755). *Nouvelle relation de la France équinoxiale.* Paris, 1743.

[90] Pierre-François-Xavier de Charlevoix (1682–1761). *Histoire de l'isle espagnole ou de S. Domingue.* Paris, 1730–1731.

[91] Nicolas Louis Bourgeois (1710?–1716?) *Voyages intéressans dans différentes colonies.* London, 1788.

[92] P. Saintard (d. ca. 1760). *Essai sur les colonies françoises.* [Paris], 1754.†

[93] France. *Lettres patentes.* Paris, 1717.

[94] France. *Arrest du Conseil d'Estat du roy, qui ordonne qu'il ne sera plus envoyé de vagabonds…à la Louisianne.* Paris, 1720.

[95] *Recueil de voyages au Nord.* Amsterdam, 1725–1738.

[96] Le Page du Pratz (d. 1775). *Histoire de Louisiane.* Paris, 1758.

[97] Dumont de Montigny. *Mémoires historiques sur la Louisiane.* Paris, 1753.

[98] Jean Bernard Bossu (1720–1792). *Nouveaux voyages aux Indes Occidentales.* Paris, 1768.

[99] Joseph François Lafitau (1681–1746). *Moeurs des sauvages amériquains.* Paris, 1724.

[100] Pehr Kalm (1716–1779). *Travels into North America.* London, 1770–1771 (translated by Johann Reinhold Forster).

[101] John Dawson Gilmary Shea (1824–1892). *Relations diverses sur la bataille de Malangueulé.* New York, 1860.

[102] *Relation de ce qui s'est passé cette année en Canada.* Paris, [1755].

[103] Louis-Antoine de Bougainville (1729–1811). *Voyage autour du monde.* Paris, 1771.

[104] Jean Baptiste Mathieu Thibault de Chanvalon (ca. 1725–1788). *Voyage à la Martinique.* Paris, 1763.

[105] Chevalier de Préfontaine. *Maison rustique.* Paris, 1763.

[106] France. *Lettres-patentes.* Lyons, 1763.

[107] Jacques Nicolas Bellin (1703–1722). *Description géographique de la Guiane.* Paris, 1763.

[108] M.D.L.S. *Dictionnaire galibi.* Paris, 1763 (variously attributed to Simon Philibert de La Salle de l'Etang and M. de La Sauvage).

[109] Bertrand Bajon (1751 – 1778). *Mémoires pour servir à l'histoire de Cayenne.* Paris, 1777.

[110] M. Guisan. *Traité, sur les terres noyées de la Guiane.* Cayenne, 1788.

[111] Michel René Hilliard d'Auberteuil (1751–1789). *Considérations sur l'état présent de la colonie française de Saint-Domingue.* Paris, 1776–1777.

[112] France. *Arrêt du Conseil d'Etat du roi, portant suppression d'un ouvrage intitulé: Considérations sur l'état présent de la colonie françoise de Saint-Domingue.* Paris, 1777.

[113] Pierre-Victor Malouet (1740–1814). *Mémoire sur l'esclavage des nègres.* Neuchâtel, 1788.‡

[114] Marie Jean Antoine Nicolas Caritat, marquis de Condorcet (1743–1794). *Réflexions sur l'esclavage des nègres.* Neuchâtel, 1781.

[115] Pierre Ulric Dubuisson (1746–1794). *Nouvelles considérations sur Saint-Domingue.* Paris, 1780.

[116] Abbé Raynal (1713–1796). *Essai sur l'administration de St. Domingue.* [Geneva], 1785.

[117] Abbé Raynal (1713–1796). *Histoire philosophique et politique des établissemens et du commerce des Européens dans les deux Indes.* Geneva, 1780.

[118] Jacques-Pierre Brissot de Warville (1754–1793). *Mémoire sur les noirs de l'Amérique septentrionale.* Paris, 1789.

[119] Médéric Louis Elie Moreau de Saint-Méry (1750–1819). *Description topographique et politique de la partie espagnole de l'isle Saint-Domingue.* Philadelphia, 1796.

[120] Alexandre-Stanislas, baron de Wimpffen. *Voyage à Saint-Domingue.* Paris, 1797.

[121] Jean Bernard Bossu (1720–1792). *Nouveaux voyages dans l'Amérique septentrionale.* Amsterdam, 1777.

[122] Jean Bochart, chevalier de Champigny (1712–ca. 1787). *La Louisiane ensanglantée.* London, 1773.

[123] François Joseph Cugnet (1720–1789). *Traité de la police.* Quebec, 1775.

[124] France. *Arrêt du Conseil d'Etat du roi, pour l'encouragement du commerce de France avec les Etats-Unis de l'Amérique.* Paris, 1788.

[125] Abbé Robin (1750–1794). *Nouveau voyage dans l'Amérique septentrionale.* Philadelphia & Paris, 1782.

[126] François Jean Chastellux (1734–1788). *Voyage de Mr. le chevalier de Chastellux en Amérique.* [Paris], 1785.

[127] Filippo Mazzei (1730–1816). *Recherches historiques et politiques sur les Etats-Unis de l'Amérique septentrionale.* Colle & Paris, 1788.

[128] Giovanni Rinaldo Carli (1720–1795). *Lettres américaines.* Boston & Paris, 1788 (translated by Jean-Baptiste Lefebvre de Villebrune).

[129] Henri Grégoire (1750–1831). *Mémoire en faveur des gens de couleur.* Paris, 1789.

[130] Julien Raimond (1743?–1802?). *Mémoire sur les causes des troubles et des désastres de la colonie de Saint-Domingue.* Paris, 1793.

[131] France. *Rapport sur les troubles de Saint-Domingue.* Paris, 1797–1799 (edited by Jean Philippe Garran de Coulon).

[132] Dubroca (1757–ca. 1835). *L'itinéraire des Français dans la Louisiane.* Paris, 1802.

[133] Nicolas Jacquemin (1736–1819). *Mémoire sur la Louisiane.* Paris, 1803.

LES NOUVELLES FRANCES

Introduction

THE FRENCH IMPACT on the shaping of the Americas has been more extensive than the casual observer may suspect. The simple exercise of counting the number of New World peoples with Gallic surnames demonstrates this fact. In Canada, there are about seven million ethnic French, or about 27 percent of the population. In the United States, according to the 1980 census, some fourteen million people bear French names, although only a minority are French speakers. In the Caribbean basin, Guadeloupe, Martinique and their dependencies as well as French Guiana have resisted the modern trend of independence from the mother country. Almost one million francophones live there. Haiti, independent since 1804, retains a Gallic flavor in its culture.

Diverse streams of migration account for the surprising number of Franco-Americans in the United States. From French Canada (New France) came explorers, fur traders (*coureurs de bois* or woodsroamers), and a small number of farmers to the Great Lakes area and the upper Mississippi Valley. Some of these pioneers migrated further south upon the establishment of Mobile (1701) and New Orleans (1718). Significant numbers of French Huguenots, stripped of their religious rights by the Revocation of the Edict of Nantes (1685), settled in English America. Among their descendants were such prominent figures in the Revolutionary era as Paul Revere, John Jay, and Frances Marion. At the end of the eighteenth century thousands of refugees, in large measure planters and royalists, fled the upheavals in France and in the Antilles, especially from the slave revolts at Saint Domingue (Haiti). They settled in Philadelphia, New Orleans, Charleston, and New York. Finally, the nineteenth and early twentieth centuries saw a flood of French-speaking migrants from Canada to the United States in search of greater economic opportunity.

The French demographic impact has been less dramatic outside the North American continent. Despite that fact, during the three centuries covered in this catalogue it was the colonies in the Caribbean that were considered the most valuable to France. In 1750, for example, some six hundred French ships visited the Antilles whereas only twenty sailed to New France and but a few dropped anchor at Cayenne, the capital of Guiana, and at Mobile and New Orleans. Using population as a measure, until the eighteenth century there were more European French in the Caribbean Islands—which except for Saint Domingue are tiny—than on the North American mainland.

This catalogue and the accompanying exhibition will therefore devote at least as much space to the Caribbean basin settlements as to the more well-known mainland colonies. In addition, significant attention will be accorded to failed colonial initiatives, such as those that had for their object "Florida" (presently Florida, Georgia, and the Carolinas), and Brazil. This hemispheric approach reflects well the magnificent French collections of the John Carter Brown Library. As strong as are the Library's holdings on the mainland colonies, its books, pamphlets, and maps relating to the Caribbean basin and South America are probably unmatched outside of France; and they include unique or nearly unique items that will be highlighted in the exhibition.

The hemispheric perspective of this catalogue allows for some useful comparisons. Although most French migrants came from Paris and the coastal regions, once in the New World they lived in lands strikingly different in terms of topography, climate, and flora and fauna. Furthermore, they lived among diverse aboriginal populations, and Frenchmen in the Caribbean basin surrounded themselves with African slaves. Just as English "Puritans" in the Caribbean differed from those of New England, so did Frenchmen in the Antilles or Guiana develop lifestyles in significant ways different from those of their brothers on the St. Lawrence. One theme, then, of this sketch of French colonies in the Americas is how divergent human and natural environments shaped emerging French communities.

Another question addressed in the following pages concerns the extent and strength of the connections between the mother country and its various offspring (stepchildren, some would say) across the Atlantic. Although the degree of metropolitan control has often been exaggerated by students of official documents, it remains true that especially after 1664 the French government exceeded its English counterpart in the stringency of imperial control. The French colonies in the Americas should not be studied in isolation.

To what extent do the holdings of the John Carter Brown Library alone permit a study of French experiences in the New World? It is evident that the history of an empire cannot be written without consulting unpublished archival materials principally available in France and at American sites such as Ottawa, Quebec, New Orleans, Fort-de-France (Martinique), and Cayenne. Nevertheless, this granted, the John Carter Brown holds one of the world's most significant collections of printed primary sources relating to the French in the Americas between 1492 and 1815. Travel books, missionary relations, legal compilations, political pamphlets, and maps form the bulk of this collection. It should be emphasized that some of these works, identified in the pages below, contain printed versions of documents that have not otherwise survived the ravages of time and political turmoil.

One goal of this catalogue is to provide the political and cultural context of the Library's printed French materials. Many of these books were the tools of empire, specifically created to support colonial initiatives or to rally support in the *métropole* for existing colonies. The following sketch of the French experiences in the Americas will be shaped largely by the issues that interested writers and mapmakers of the first French colonial empire. To provide a context for understanding this literature of empire, a traditional, chronological approach is employed. With only a few exceptions, all of the primary sources cited herein are in the Library's collection.

Special thanks are due to my colleagues James Pritchard, Patricia Galloway, and David Geggus, whose reading of the manuscript has helped to minimize errors of fact. Any remaining difficulties in this respect as well as in the area of interpretation are attributable to the author's limitations. Norman Fiering, director and librarian at the John Carter Brown Library, Susan Danforth, assistant librarian, and the Library's kind and helpful staff have provided splendid support of this project. Thanks to Joan Haynes for her patience in the typing of the manuscript.

CHAPTER I

Approaches to America, 1500–1626

ALTHOUGH FRANCE did not succeed in establishing permanent colonies in the Americas during the sixteenth century, her response to the sensational news of a newfound world was more dramatic than in any other country north of the Alps. As early as 1493 there was printed in Paris an edition of Columbus's famous letter describing his first voyage. Soon thereafter, French fishermen became increasingly active along the North American coast. Some of them even brought back the "wild men" who so fascinated and horrified European observers. Far more so than the strangely uninterested English, the French reading public devoured the tales of Vespucci, Magellan, Cortés, and other Italo-Iberian heroes. Available to these readers were Hernán Cortés's *Des marches, îles et pays trouvés* (Antwerp, 1522) [1], Pietro Martire d'Anghiera's *Extraict...des isles nouvellement trouvées* (Paris, 1532) [2], and *Le Nouveau Monde et navigacions faites par Emeric de Vespuce* (Paris, 1516) [3]. These authors created an image of the New World that emphasized its fabulous mineral riches and, especially in the case of the Renaissance Italians Vespucci and Martyr (Martire), its strange but not unamiable aborigines. Trans-

lations of Spanish accounts of the conquests of the golden cities of America, especially Gonzalo Fernández de Oviedo's *L'histoire naturelle et géneralle des Indes* (Paris, 1556) [4], fascinated French readers. Popular cosmographers like Pierre Apian (*La cosmographie*, Antwerp, 1544) [5] and especially Sebastian Münster (*La cosmographie universelle*, [Basel], 1568) [6] distilled and diffused these impressions to an audience eager for exotic curiosities.

Quite unconnected with these literary conceptions, French fishermen, traders, and corsairs plied American waters in surprisingly large numbers. As early as the first decade of the century, Norman and Breton boats conducted annual fishing voyages to the Newfoundland area, and they occasionally brought back *sauvages* (the generic term for Amerindians and Eskimos) to pique the curiosity of their countrymen. Further south, swarms of French corsairs carried the Habsburg-Valois struggle to the Caribbean. To the southeast along the Brazilian coast, French shippers conducted a lively trade in brazilwood and other tropical commodities. To manage relations with Amerindians who cut and hauled the trees, French boys (*truche-*

L'IMPRIMEVR
aux Lecteurs.

SALVT.

MESSIEURS ayant ces iours passez imprimé l'Edict du Roy, contenant le pouuoir & Commission donnee par sa Maiesté au sieur Marquis de la Roche pour la conqueste des Terres-neufues, de Norembergue, Hauchelage, Canadas, Labrador, la grand' Baye, & terres adiacentes. Il m'est du depuis tombé entre les mains vn Discours du voyage fait ausdites terres, par le Capitaine Iaques Cartier, escrit en langue estrangere que i'ay fait traduire en la nostre, par vn de mes amis. I'ay pensé qu'il ne seroit hors de propos de le mettre en lu-

A ij

Fig. 1.1 "L'imprimeur aux lecteurs" from Jacques Cartier, *Discours du voyage* (1598). The publisher explains his motive for offering the readers this translation of Cartier's account of his first Canadian voyage; it is to promote the Marquis de la Roche's exclusive commission to conquer these new lands.

ments) were left in America to learn aboriginal languages and to act as agent-factors. Indeed, so intimate were relations between the French and the Tupi-Namba in particular that other Europeans in Brazil at the time, like the famous traveler-writer Hans Staden, claimed to be French to avoid the boiling pot. In France itself in 1550, veterans of the Brazil trade donned Tupi "dress" and body paint and, with the help of fifty aborigines, created a sensational *spectacle* for Henri II and Catherine de Médici upon their *entrée* to Rouen. They fought a battle *à la sauvage* for the impressed sovereigns.

These energetic commercial-corsair thrusts did not have colonizing intent; hence, they barely left a literary legacy. These intrepid entrepreneurs neither hoped to attract settlers nor wished to advertise their economic successes to potential rivals. However, even the incomplete record of their adventures demonstrates that France possessed the ships, sailors, knowledge, and courage to transplant colonies across the Atlantic—if she so wished.

If she so wished! To understand the motives behind the three sixteenth-century colonial enterprises (Cartier-Roberval in Canada, Villegaignon in Brazil, and Ribaut-Laudonnière in "Florida") is to look backwards in time and not forward to New France and New England. The intention of these expeditions was to imitate the Spanish pattern of exploration, conquest, and exploitation of land and aborigines. The search for golden cities and for dense populations of aboriginal serfs galvanized the energies of these would-be conquistadors.

From the 1520s the French king, Francis I, supported the search for a Northwest Passage to the Orient. In 1524 Giovanni Verrazano sailed the coast of North America in search of the anticipated opening. His failure to find the route to Cathay and the king's Italian wars caused a ten-year delay before Jacques Cartier's first voyage. Francis authorized Cartier in 1534 to search for "certain islands and countries where it is said there are great quantities of gold," undoubtedly a reference to Cortés's now-famous triumphs. Cartier's *Discours du voyage* [7] was later printed at Rouen in 1598. His second voyage of 1536, during which he wintered at future Quebec city, reported Amerindian tales of the golden city called Saguenay. The interest in France kindled by these voyages led the king to support the Cartier-Roberval colonial expedition of 1541–1542. Cartier returned to Quebec where after spending a difficult winter he decided to sail for France with a cargo of what he believed was gold and diamonds. The slow-moving Roberval was just arriving. The fact that Cartier's minerals were worthless (leading to the popular saying "fake as a Canadian diamond") and the failure of Roberval to plant a colony or discover Saguenay discouraged further colonizing expeditions before 1598.

The composition of the Cartier-Roberval expedition underlines its true motivation. Francis I's stated purpose was to convert the aborigines to Catholicism, a goal he believed might secure papal approval of this explicit encroachment on Spain's claim to monopoly of the New World. But this purpose appears somewhat rhetorical since Roberval was a Huguenot nobleman and no missionaries sailed with the expedition. Roberval attracted a number of adventurers, particularly impoverished nobles, whose imaginations were undoubtedly fired by Cortés's well-publicized triumphs. For the bulk of the personnel, however, the leaders had to resort to prisoners, perhaps because of the opposition of the Atlantic seaports to schemes that smacked of official interference in the fisheries. Hardly any artisans or peasants shipped with Roberval. The hazards of winter trauma and scurvy aside, success was

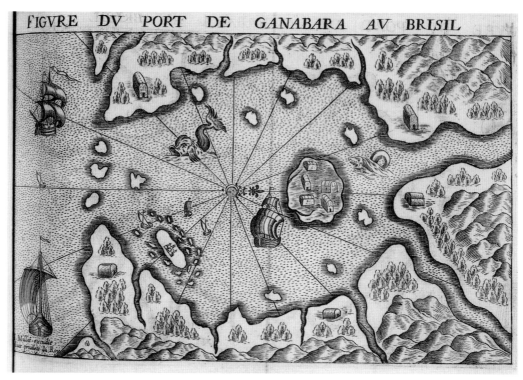

FIGVRE DV PORT DE GANABARA AV BRISIL

Fig. 1.2 "Port de Ganabara au Brésil" from Marc Lescarbot, *Histoire de la Nouvelle France* (1609).
A sketch of Guanabara Bay with Villegaignon's settlement on Guanabara Island, the largest one in the bay. The Portuguese destruction of the colony (1565) led to the founding of Rio de Janeiro on the opposite mainland.

thus dependent on the ability of French military might to coerce labor from the Iroquoian groups on the St. Lawrence. But these powerful peoples, already strongly alienated by Cartier's previous kidnappings, not only prevented such enforced labor; they made hazardous any attempted explorations in search of Saguenay and China.

The Villegaignon expedition to Brazil in 1555 must be understood within its political and diplomatic context. Brazil was incontestably the most well-known part of America in sixteenth-century France. Besides the popular Vespucci, the companion of Magellan, Antonio Pigafetta, described the Brazilian coast in his *Le voyage et navigation* (Paris, [1525]) [8], the first published account of the round-the-world expedition. As noted above, French traders were thoroughly familiar

Cõme ce peuple couppe et porte le Bresil és nauires.

Fig. 1.3 "Come ce peuple couppe" from André Thevet, *La cosmographie universelle* (1575).

The Brazilwood trade attracted French ships to Brazil throughout the sixteenth century. Dependence on indigenous labor explains in large measure the benign French conduct toward the coastal aborigines.

with the coast and its aborigines, and Montaigne's famous essay "Cannibals" is one indication that their knowledge was diffused in the mother country.

At least since 1546, Portuguese warships had tried to force French compliance with the Treaty of Tordesillas (1494), which granted Brazil to Portugal. Then in the 1550s, the Valois-Habsburg struggle reached a pinnacle of intensity, which undoubtedly helps to explain Henri II's (1547–1559) and the Admiral Gaspard de Coligny's support of Villegaignon's venture. Nevertheless, much remains obscure about Villegaignon's motives. Were his fortifications at Guanabara (near present-day Rio de Janeiro) intended for defense against Portuguese attacks or as bastions from which to sally forth against the Iberians? Why did he choose a spot so

Fig. 1.4 "La Floride" from Marc Lescarbot, *Histoire de la Nouvelle France* (1611). Lescarbot, who had not visited "Florida," based this map on French accounts of the 1560s expeditions. Charlesfort, Port Royal, the site of the first French settlement (present-day Parris Island, South Carolina) is at the top right. Fort Caroline is at the R. de May (St. John's River), which has its reputed source in a "great lake" to the northwest. The actual headwaters are almost due south.

far to the south? Did he intend to carve out a feudal kingdom? If so, why the all-male composition of his party?

Despite repeated assertions in later accounts that Villegaignon engaged in a Huguenot enterprise, the facts suggest otherwise. Henri II, who unwillingly tolerated Calvinism in France only because of the struggle with Spain, would hardly have supported with some ten thousand *livres* an overtly Protestant settlement. Although sympathetic to the Huguenots in 1555, Coligny declared publicly for their cause only in 1558. Little evidence supports later Huguenot assertions that Villegaignon was a Calvinist in 1555 only to turn traitor in Brazil. He was, after all, a Knight of Malta and friend of the powerful and ultra-Catholic Guise family. Estimates are that only one-

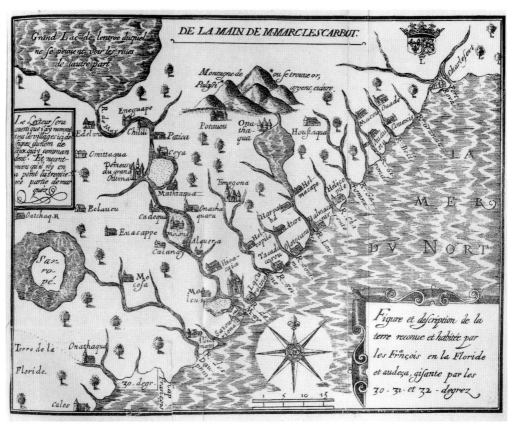

third of his party were of Calvinist inclinations, and the remaining recruits had to be sought in the prisons. It was for the purpose of enticing better colonists that from Brazil Villegaignon appealed to his old acquaintance from University of Paris days, John Calvin, to send colonists to his *La France antarctique*.

Arriving at present-day Rio de Janeiro, Villegaignon chose to build his fortified settlement on the island of Guanabara, two miles off the coast, apparently to ensure his control over the prisoner element and to prevent the colonists from "association and familiarity with the unbelievers." The autocratic and puritanical leader demanded long and heavy labor from the colonists and quarantined them from the aborigines. Perhaps influenced by Vespucci's fantastic descriptions of free love in the tropics, Villegaignon feared that the sexual allure of peoples he considered hardly more than animals would cause the disintegration of his community and undermine his authority. Inevitably, these policies promoted murmurings and even desertions to the mainland. It was at an increasingly troubled colony that Calvin's envoys arrived.

Much remains unclear about the events that followed and especially who was to blame. It appears that after a period of initial friendship a bitter dispute arose between the amateur theologian Villegaignon and the Genevans on the issue of transubstantiation, the Catholic doctrine of the corporeal transformation of the bread and wine at the Mass into the body and blood of Jesus Christ. The outcome was the expulsion of the Calvinists to the mainland and thence to Europe.

These doctrinal fissures doomed the colony. After having caused this division in the colony, Villegaignon sailed to France in 1559 with sundry curiosities and fifty *sauvages*, ostensibly to recruit reenforcements but also to protect his good name against Huguenot attacks. Whatever had previously been his religious leaning, Villegaignon now demonstrated his orthodoxy by approaching the Jesuits for support of the colony. However, he never found an expedient time to return to Brazil, perhaps because Henri II had lost interest. As the religious passions between Catholics and Huguenots heated up, Villegaignon wrote pamphlets defending his conduct in Brazil and, after 1562, fought until his death on the Catholic side of the religious wars (1560–1594).

Following Villegaignon's departure from Guanabara, the remnants of the colony succumbed to a Portuguese assault. Frightened by this blatant French and Calvinist invasion of their claimed territories, the Portuguese moved rapidly to develop Brazil. Thus ended the major sixteenth-century French colonial effort in South America; what did not end, however, was the extensive French-aborigines trade. The polemics concerning Villegaignon also continued, as we will see.

No doubt disgusted by the dénouement of the Brazilian affair, the now openly Huguenot Coligny looked for other weak points in the Iberian New World empire. In 1562, he sponsored the first "Florida" voyage to establish a fortified place athwart the crucial shipping lanes of Spanish America. If this action provoked a renewal of war with Spain, at peace with France since the Treaty of Cateau-Cambrésis (1559), then such a conflict might unite embittered French Catholics and Huguenots. Philip II of Spain, the most powerful sovereign in Europe, could ill-afford to ignore this challenge to his treasure routes.

The noted Huguenot captain Jean Ribaut of Dieppe, Coligny's choice to lead the initial reconnaissance, selected a secluded spot off the South Carolina coast (Parris Island) for his Port Royal colony, and left some twenty-five men there. Returning to France for reenforcements, Ribaut got caught up in

Fig. 1.5 Map of Fort Caroline
from *Coppie d'une lettre venant
de la Floride envoyée à Rouen*
(1565). (Enlarged).
This rare account of the second
French expedition to "Florida"
(1564) presents a sketch of
Fort Caroline at the St. John's
river near present-day Jacksonville, Florida. Notice the
strange, serpentine shape of a
river without headwaters.

the outbreak of religious war in France. After forced exile to England, he published an account of his "Florida" voyage, the *Whole & true discoverye of Terra Florida* (London, 1563) [9]. Meanwhile at Port Royal, the colonists demonstrated how mentally entrapped they were by the hated Spaniards' perceptions of America. Expecting to be fed by the local inhabitants, the French searched for the fabled city of Cibola where gold and gems were strewn on the ground. Inflamed by the occasional gold ornaments that the aborigines had retrieved from Spanish shipwrecks, these would-be conquistadors thrashed about in search of elusive treasure even as their provisions rapidly dwindled. Before total disaster occurred, they struggled home in a hastily constructed craft.

In 1564, after a truce in France temporarily halted religious fratricide, Coligny asked Ribaut's lieutenant on the first voyage, René de Laudonnière, to lead a second expedition. A sketch of this voyage is found in the rare *Coppie d'une lettre venant de la Floride envoyée à Rouen* (Paris, 1565) [10]. The subsequent establishment of a colony near Jacksonville, Florida (Fort Caroline) and its brutal extirpation by the Spanish captain-general Menéndez de Avilés became the subject of numerous Huguenot polemics. Modern historians of Spanish Florida have provided correctives to the Huguenot version of events, and an accurate sketch now seems possible.

Troubles plagued Laudonnière's settlement almost from the beginning. Disdaining agriculture, and thus dependent on the native inhabitants, the colonists had to assist their Amerindian allies in local conflicts. Laudonnière also found it impossible to control the wanderlust of his gold-hungry men. Failure to discover mineral riches and the increasing inability of the Amerindian allies to grant provisions led to growing dis-

sension. A group of desperadoes forced Laudonnière to permit a privateering venture to the Caribbean, and it was their capture that alerted Spanish authorities to the French colony's site. As conditions at Fort Caroline deteriorated, Laudonnière reluctantly agreed to abandon the colony. At that critical juncture, the famous English corsair John Hawkins visited the colony on his return from the Caribbean. He graciously provided food and a ship for the colonists' return, in exchange for the fort's cannon. Laudonnière was thus able to persuade the men to wait a little longer for expected reenforcements.

In France, Jean Ribaut had returned from exile, and with Coligny's aid recruited a large force of some six hundred colonists, including for the first time women and children. The religious tensions of the era apparently made it possible to recruit settlers without having to turn to prisons. Time was lost in preparations, and unwarranted delays occurred along the Florida coast. As a consequence, Ribaut arrived at Fort Caroline only six days before the imperial avenger, Menéndez de Avilés. The intrepid Ribaut soon attacked the Spanish fleet, only to have his ships dispersed by winds of hurricane intensity. Seizing his advantage, Menéndez organized a quick and decisive Spanish march that surprised a weak and unprepared Fort Caroline, and only a handful of French soldiers, including the sick Laudonnière, escaped. Some fifty women and children were spared. Proceeding to the Matanzas Inlet, the Spaniards caught the survivors of Ribaut's wrecked ships and massacred most of them after, according to dubious Huguenot testimony, allegedly promising leniency. In subsequent years, Menéndez founded Saint Augustine and fortified other places on the coast to prevent further French incursions. So ended the largest and most promising French colonial venture on the North American mainland in the sixteenth century.

These accounts of the Canada, Brazil, and "Florida" expeditions all lead to the same conclusion: that sixteenth-century French colonial failures are partly attributable to the stranglehold that Spanish conceptions of New World conquest and exploitation had on the French imagination. French adventurers were determined to emulate the great Spanish conquistadors, or failing that, to loot the Spanish looters. However, the French adventurers did not find concentrated aboriginal populations like the Aztecs to exploit, and their insensitive treatment of potential allies and trading partners left them in untenable positions. Without assistance from the Indians, the French were vulnerable to fierce Iberian counterattacks in Brazil and "Florida" that easily uprooted the shallowly planted colonies.

Most historians pass quickly over the years between 1565 and the opening of the Canadian trading posts after 1600, asserting that the era of bitter religious strife averted attention from the New World. While not inaccurate, this view ignores the established and continuing patterns of activity by French traders, raiders, and sailors. Fishing fleets continued their annual runs, and the dry fishers (those who cured their catch on shore before the return to France) traded for furs with the aborigines at Newfoundland. Dyewood traders continued to visit Brazil, and they supplied guns to the Tupi-Namba to resist Portuguese slavers. *Truchements* eased this trade and often organized native defenses against the increasingly powerful Portuguese. French corsairs, in smaller numbers than earlier, joined a growing number of English raiders in the Spanish Caribbean. Not a few of these French ships proceeded to points along the Florida-Georgia-Carolina coast to trade for sassafras and sarsparilla with the locals. In short, traditional mercantile and corsair activities continued after 1565, albeit somewhat less intensely.

Despite a probable decrease of French forays in America, the number of literary accounts of the New World dramatically increased after 1565, principally because of Catholic-Huguenot polemics concerning the Brazil and "Florida" fiascoes. Between 1565 and 1610 over one hundred French works contained information about the Americas, about five times greater than the number of accounts prior to 1565. But interest in the establishment of overseas colonies—never very strong—became utterly subordinate to historical arguments about what might have been.

Translations of the great Spanish accounts of the New World in the second half of the sixteenth century usually served partisan purposes while providing information and entertainment. The numerous editions of Francisco López de Gómara's *Histoire générale des Indes Occidentales* (Paris, 1605; many earlier printings) [11] portrayed the "Indies" as a Spanish preserve, glorified the conquistadors, and maligned most Amerindians. The Hispanophile views of Gómara and his great predecessor Oviedo [4] were distilled and spread by many cosmographies, especially those printed in French at Spanish-held Antwerp. These works, which include Abraham Ortelius's *Théâtre de l'univers* (Antwerp, 1598) [12] and Peeter Heyns's *Le miroir du monde* (Antwerp, 1579) [13], undoubtedly found a reading audience among Spain's Catholic friends in France, who had come to view the colonial endeavors in Brazil and "Florida" as a Huguenot conspiracy. These Catholic concerns would long cast suspicion on those advocating renewed colonial initiatives.

French translations of Spanish works were

also published in support of international Calvinism. Most famous were the numerous translations of the Spanish Bishop Las Casas's *Brevissima relacion*, which described and denounced his countrymen's brutal exploitation of the aborigines. In his translation of Las Casas's work entitled *Tyrannies et cruautéz des Espagnols* (Rouen, 1630 and many earlier printings) [14], Jacques Miggrode pointedly warned Frenchmen to be on their guard unless they wished to suffer the Indians' fate. The Italian Girolamo Benzoni, a veteran of many years in Spanish America, confirmed Las Casas's account of Spanish cruelties. The prominent Huguenot Urbain Chauveton translated Benzoni's work as *Histoire nouvelle du Nouveau Monde* ([Geneva], 1579) [15].

When Frenchmen pondered the meaning of the Brazil and "Florida" episodes, their conclusions were polemical and divisive. Shortly after the "Florida" debacle a survivor, Nicolas Le Challeux, set forth the Huguenot point of view in his popular *Discours de l'histoire de la Floride* (Dieppe, 1566) [16]. This simple carpenter's narrative culminated with a vivid account of the Matanzas Inlet tragedy. Although not an eyewitness, having escaped with Laudonnière from Fort Caroline, Le Challeux's account of the Matanzas massacre included the grotesque but probably fictive story of the shipment of Ribaut's head as a trophy of war for Philip II. Exhibiting scant interest in reviving French colonization in Florida, Le Challeux wrote instead to ignite a national outburst of indignation against Spain. If so, the Court took little heed of this and other protests. Charles IX and the Queen Mother Catherine de Médici gave a cool reception to the survivors and were furious at the Catholic Captain Dominique de Gourgues, who led an unauthorized attack against weakly defended Spanish forts in Florida in 1567, as an act of revenge. (See his *Histoire mémorable de la reprinse de l'isle de la Floride*, [Paris], 1568) [17].

The trumpeted raid of de Gourgues seems to have cooled partisan tempers about America until the monk André Thevet reopened the wounds with his *Cosmographie universelle* (Paris, 1575) [18]. After a short stay at Villegaignon's settlement, Thevet had published his *Singularitéz de la France antarctique* (Paris, 1558) [19] before the troubles at Guanabara. In that popular book, Thevet painted a general, rather superficial picture of the environment and a portrait of the *sauvages* that emphasized their exotic if brutal customs. In his *Cosmographie*, however, Thevet stoked the flames of religious animosity by blaming the Calvinists and their "bloody Gospel" for the Brazilian failure. In that same year, 1575, François de Belleforest translated Sebastian Münster's popular work as *La cosmographie´universelle* (Paris, 1575) [20], but he also added materials on Brazil and Florida. He asserted that Calvinist emigrants "from the abysmal hell of Geneva" sabotaged Villegaignon's authority and hence destroyed the colony.

The Huguenots were not long in answering these challenges. Jean de Léry's *Histoire d'un voyage fait en . . . Brésil* ([La Rochelle], 1578; four later editions) [21] was the most effective rebuttal and, furthermore, provided the most favorable sixteenth-century French view of the Amerindians. Dismissing Thevet as "an ignorant author" who committed frequent and gross errors, Léry attacked Villegaignon for luring the Calvinists with a promise of religious freedom, and then reneging after receiving a letter of reproach from the powerful Cardinal of Lorraine, a Guise. The commandant then persecuted the Calvinists and thus fatally weakened *la France antarctique*. What a tragedy, since Léry

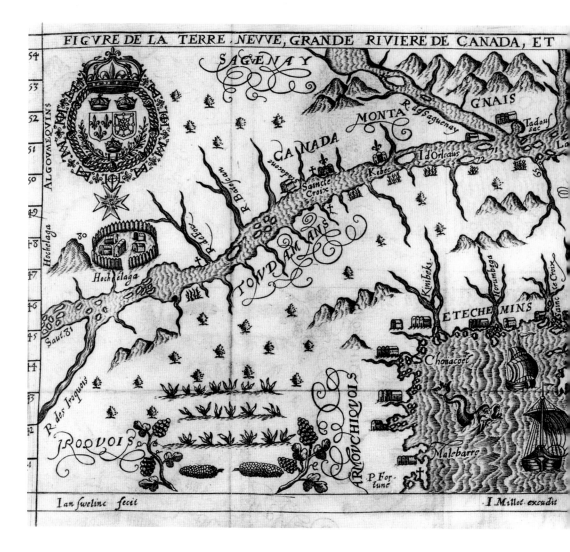

found much to admire about the land and especially its peoples. Was not their nakedness much less offensive than that of half-clothed court women? Was not their custom of man-eating less horrifying than instances of Catholic cannibalism during the Religious Wars? With Léry (and Montaigne) was born the French version of the exemplary savage. Look what nature alone, without the help of divine grace, can produce and then compare it with the vulgarities of reputedly civilized, Christian life.

Among many other Huguenots entering the ideological fray, Voisin de La Popelinière

(*Les trois mondes*, Paris, 1582) [22] publicized Le Challeux's shocking account of the Spanish treatment of Ribaut's skull. La Popelinière also helped the cause by making available Laudonnière's *Histoire notable de la Floride* (Paris, 1586) [23]. Laudonnière justified his account by the need to extirpate the "lies" then current about the events of 1564–1565. Urbain Chauveton attached Le Challeux's *Discours* [16] to his translation of Benzoni, and in the introduction lambasted Thevet for "deep ignorance of history and cosmography."

The Huguenot propaganda campaign

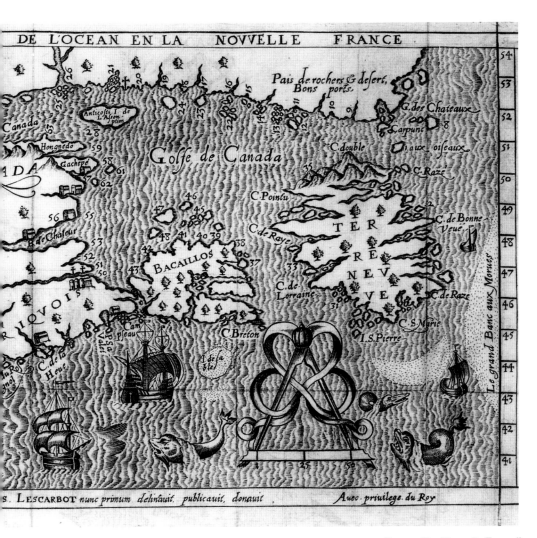

Fig. 1.6 "La Nouvelle France" from Marc Lescarbot, *Histoire de la Nouvelle France* (1609). Lescarbot accompanied Champlain up the St. Lawrence in 1608. The map shows "Kébec" at Hochelaga and also reflects the extensive French activities in Acadia (Nova Scotia and Northern Maine).

reached its crescendo as the last Valois, Henri III, suffered assassination (1588) and was replaced by the Huguenot leader Henri IV, the first Bourbon. Not only Huguenots but moderate Catholics expressed outrage over Spanish barbarism in the New World. Nevertheless, the Catholic versus Huguenot propaganda dispute of these years was an inhibiting factor in colonial development. For the Huguenots, rehashing the Brazil and "Florida" episodes could yield important advantages, but few of these authors argued for new endeavors overseas. Le Challeux, for example, pointedly warned fellow Calvinists that God had punished the Florida colonists "for abandoning our families." With their former leader Henri IV on the throne, the Huguenots' place was in France to protect their religious freedoms (formally protected with the Edict of Nantes, 1598). At the same time, fervent Catholics opposed French overseas excursions as an intrusion into their Spanish ally's American empire.

One important legacy of these failed colonial expeditions was the development of a stereotype of the French national character. Daring and brilliant in the execution of difficult projects like exploration and conquest, the French were allegedly too impatient to stay the long and tedious course of colonial development. Montaigne feared that "we have eyes bigger than our stomachs and more curiosity than capacity for colonization." Henri IV's minister Sully warned that the French regretfully "do not have either the perseverance or the foresight" to build overseas settlements. These sentiments were to be endlessly repeated in the seventeenth century and undoubtedly acted as self-fulfilling prophecies. Even Cardinal Richelieu, an advocate of colonization, became resigned to the mercurial French character. Colonial proponents would battle against these concepts with little apparent effect.

With the advent of peace with Spain (Treaty of Vervins, 1598) and the diminution of religious conflict at home, Henri IV gave support to new mercantile and colonial endeavors. He chartered the French East Indies Company in order to join forces with the Dutch assault on the Iberians. He acted to revitalize the Levant trade and to prevent attacks on French shipping by corsairs. His support of French endeavors in North America was somewhat lukewarm, however, perhaps because he feared reawakening Catholic-Huguenot distrust. Nevertheless, the king was unwilling to abandon French

rights to exploit unoccupied lands, as demonstrated by the loud silence in the Treaty of Vervins on the issue of Spanish claims to monopoly in the New World. Thus, the French editor of the magnificent *Histoire naturelle et morale des Indes* by the Spanish Jesuit José de Acosta (Paris, 1616; first edition, 1598) [24] could be assured that his dedication to the king would receive a friendly reception. This translation was explicitly intended to serve as a French guide to Spanish territories overseas.

The publisher of Cartier's *Discours du voyage* in Rouen in 1598 [7] expressed the hope that it would support the Marquis de la Roche's expedition of that year. The increasing mercantile interest in the fur trade led Henri IV to grant monopoly concessions to companies in return for underwriting colonial development. In 1603, in return for transporting six hundred colonists, he granted Acadia (Northern Maine, Nova Scotia) and its fur trade to the Huguenot de Monts and his La Rochelle associates for ten years. The company's monopoly, however, elicited a cacophony of protests from affected coastal interests, and the king rescinded it in 1607. Thus began a pattern of such royal grants followed by organized private resistance and overt disobedience. Bereft of the Acadian concession, de Monts commissioned his able lieutenant, the royal captain Samuel de Champlain, to establish a trading post at Quebec. Meanwhile the Huguenot de Poutrincourt created a post at Port Royal (later Annapolis) in Nova Scotia.

In the decades after 1608, Champlain established the policies that would guide the colony of New France during much of the seventeenth century. He advocated French emigration to the St. Lawrence to promote a stable, agricultural community. Alliances were forged with neighboring Algonkian nations (Ottawas, Montagnais, etc.) and with the Iroquoian-speaking Hurons to assure a supply of furs for export. Inevitably, this policy entailed French military support of Indian allies in their wars, notably against the five Iroquois nations that controlled the area west of Lake Champlain and south of Lakes Erie and Ontario.

One of the major results of these Canadian initiatives was the emergence of a literature that advocated French colonial development. Previously the author of a manuscript account of his voyage to Spanish Mexico (the John Carter Brown Library owns this unique work) [25], Champlain published in 1603 a short description of his voyage to Acadia with de Monts. *Des sauvages, ou, voyage* (Paris, [1603]) [26] presents his first, and none too positive, impressions of the purportedly bestial, nomadic peoples encountered there. More relevant to the development of a viable colonial plan was Marc Lescarbot's *Histoire de la Nouvelle France* (Paris, 1609 and later expanded editions) [27]. In a long analysis of previous French misadventures overseas, the Parisian lawyer chided his countrymen for their lack of patience for such difficult tasks. The conquistadorlike rummaging about for golden cities and the transfer of religious discords across the Atlantic had undermined these endeavors. As to the present and future, Lescarbot painted a glowing portrait of the fertility and resources of Canada. Prisoner, pauper, and peasant would discover there the opportunities so lacking at home. The author attacked frontally the popular image of a cruel, disease-ridden, and wintry land inhabited by irredeemable *sauvages*. Colonists must expect to work hard at making the land yield its riches, and at all costs the quixotic searches for the North American equivalents of El Dorado—Cibola, Norumbega, Saguenay—must be discouraged. "The most beautiful mine that I know of is wheat and wine, with feed for beasts. He

who has these, he has silver. We do not live by mines." The colony could profit greatly from trade with the *sauvages* who, with the exception of the barbarous Iroquois, love the French. This quintessentially "mercantilist" conception of the value of colonies would long influence proponents of French overseas expansion.

Continued Huguenot influence in the New World was evident in reconnaissance voyages to northern South America from the Amazon to the Orinoco, the no-man's-land between the Iberian settlements. Henri IV sponsored an expedition in 1604 led by the Huguenot vice-admiral of Brittany, La Ravardière. Whatever information is available about this voyage is found in the *Voyages en Afrique, Asie, Indes Orientales, & Occidentales* (Rouen, 1645) [28] of Jean Mocquet, who joined the exploring party as curator of the king's "cabinet of curiosities." Three years later in 1607, La Ravardière constructed a post at Cayenne (French Guiana), which quickly succumbed to disease and attacks by the Carib-speaking Galibis. France's traditional interest in the dyewood trade undoubtedly motivated the search for a region unoccupied by the Portuguese. Perhaps, also, the European fascination with El Dorado enticed the king and La Ravardière. No doubt, too, the French were becoming aware of the sugar boom of northern Brazil (see among others François Pyrard de Laval's *Voyage* [Paris, 1619]) [29]. Finally, a French colony strategically placed between Brazil and "Peru" would threaten Philip III, monarch of Spain and Portugal, in the probable resumption of war.

The sudden death by assassination of Henri IV (1610) did not discourage La Ravardière. He proposed a colonial expedition to the island of Maragnan (São Luis de Maranhão) near the mouth of the Amazon, an area which was the final refuge from Portuguese persecution of the perennial French

allies, the Tupi-Namba. But La Ravardière had to gain the support of the regent and Queen Mother Marie de Médici. A fervent Catholic, Marie and the young Louis XIII ruled at a time of growing revitalization of the Catholic Church in France. To obtain Marie's approval, La Ravardière secured the support of the devoutly Catholic François de Razilly, who in turn requested missionaries from the Capuchin (reformed Franciscan) house at Paris.

An expedition in 1612 established a settlement at Maragnan, to which was attracted the scattered and demoralized Tupi-Namba bands. After four months, Razilly and a sick Capuchin Claude d'Abbeville returned to France in search of money and colonists.

OPPOSITE:
Fig. 1.7 Missionaries, from Claude, d'Abbeville, *Histoire de la mission des pères capucins* (1614). (Enlarged).
The French commander François de Razilly and the Capuchin missionaries plant the Cross among the worshipful Tupi-Namba at Maragnan (São Luís de Maranhão). Notice the tents (not used by the Brazilians) in the background.

Fig. 1.8 "Louis de St Iehan" from Claude, d'Abbeville, *Histoire de la mission des pères capucins* (1614).
One of the six Tupi-Namba that the organizers of the 1612 expedition brought to France to elicit support. How they enchanted a Paris avid for curiosities! It was perhaps in this costume that Louis de St. Jehan appeared before young Louis XIII.

OVERLEAF:
Fig. 1.9 "Le Canada" by Champlain (1653).
This map by Champlain reflects his extensive reconnaissances into the North American interior. Notice the southern extension of Hudson Bay and the short distance between Cape Cod and Chesapeake Bay.

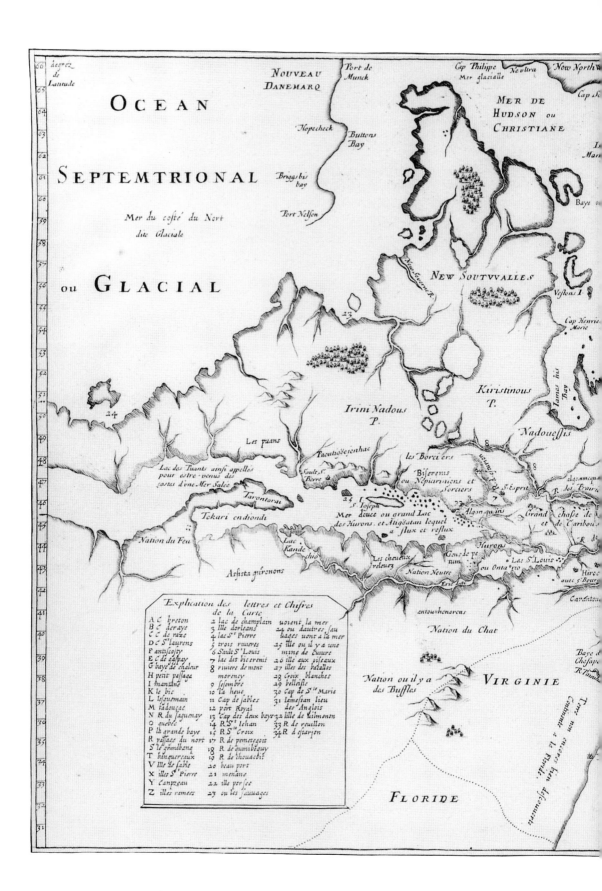

OCEAN

SEPTEMTRIONAL

*Mer du costé du Nort
dite Glaciale*

ou GLACIAL

NOUVEAU
DANEMARQ

*Port de
Munck*

Hopecheek

*Buttons
Bay*

*Briggs bis
bay*

Port Nelson

Cap Philipe   Neutra   New North W

Mer glacialle

MER DE
HUDSON ou
CHRISTIANE

Cap Se

Baye ou

Nieu Gouernor R.

NEW SOUTVVALLES

Veslons I.

*Cap Henrie
Marie*

23

Kiristinous
P.

Nadoueßis

24

Les puans

Irini Nadous
P.

*Lac des Puants ainsi apellés
pour estre venus des
costes d'vne Mer Salée*

Taoutioßejenhac

les Borci ers

8

*Saults St.
Pierre*

Biserenis
ou Nipiarinicns et
Sorciers

Algomequ.ins

St. Esprit

R. des Prair.

7

Tarontorut

25

Ioseph

Algon qu ins

Grand   chasse
et   de Caribou.

Tekari endiondi

*Mer douce ou grand Lac
des Hurons, et Augsatan lequel
a flux et reflux*

Hurons

R. de

Nation du Feu

*Lac
Kande
chio*

Les cheueux
releuex

Gou. de ve
nim.

Nation Neutre

Eric Lac

Lac St. Louis
ou Onta °rio

Hirec
auec St. Bour

Ashsta guronons

antouxhenerens

Cardatiou

Nation du Chat

Nation ou il y a
des Buffles

VIRGINIE

*Baye d
Chesap*

R. Patuan

FLORIDE

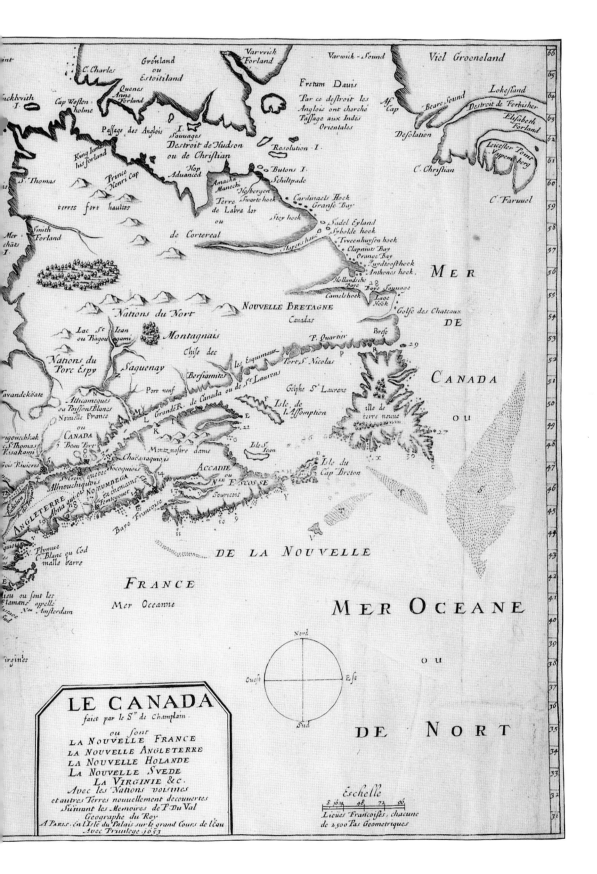

Aided by six Tupi-Namba who excited great curiosity in Paris, Razilly and Father Claude choreographed a propaganda pageant. The *sauvages* formally addressed the young king, received the baptismal waters amidst a huge throng, and the three who survived France's climate and diseases married very willing girls. The *Toupinamboux* were the talk of the town.

This publicity campaign also included a literary blitz. Ultimately fifteen books and pamphlets, of which the John Carter Brown Library has eight, were published. Most important are Claude's *Histoire de la mission des pères capucins* (Paris, 1614) [30] and the *Suitte de l'histoire des choses plus mémorables* (Paris, 1615) [31] by his fellow Capuchin Yves d'Evreux. They articulated what became the classic missionary-colonial thesis. In their vision, Maragnan was a fertile field for evangelization because the Tupi-Namba were by nature simple peoples. Unspoiled by private property and its associated ills, the *sauvages* were often more virtuous than many Christians. They were receptive to the French and especially respectful of the reverend fathers, who after all lived much as they did in simplicity and communality.

Why therefore was a colony necessary for their evangelization? To force the Tupi-Namba to abandon awful customs like cannibalism and polygamy, which the fathers blamed generally on original sin and more specifically on the Tupi-Namba contact with the devil and alcohol. A colony would provide a good Christian example to these people and protect them from their Portuguese tormentors. To attract French settlers, the Capuchins depicted Maragnan as just this side of the terrestrial paradise; in the words of Claude d'Abbeville, "the beauty and delights of this land and its fertility and fecundity are all that a man could desire for the contentment and recreation of his body."

Thus was established the critical link between evangelization and colonization. Because subsequent Capuchins, Jesuits, Dominicans, and Recollects were often writing at the behest of expedition leaders, colonial companies, and even government ministers, these missionary authors could hardly question the assumed link between colonization and conversion.

Despite Razilly's recruitment of perhaps two hundred colonists, the Maragnan project failed. Alerted by the publicity, the Portuguese attacked the colony in 1614. The French resisted successfully through 1615, but in that year all hopes of reenforcement ceased when the Queen Mother sacrificed Maragnan to her son's Spanish marriage. Among the immediate victims of the Regent's abandonment of Brazil was Yves d'Evreux's book, because only a few copies survived the orders to destroy it.

La Ravardière held onto Maragnan until the capitulation of 1616, but no one could doubt that Portugal had struck a knockdown blow in the long struggle against French traders and interlopers. France's interest in the Amazon as a highway to Peru and as a shortcut to El Dorado would continue during the seventeenth century, but in general the level of French activity along the Brazilian coast dropped rapidly after 1616.

The first years of the Regency were nearly as disastrous for New France. Before Henri IV's death, Jesuits had received permission to establish themselves at Acadia, but their departure for the area had been strongly opposed by Poutrincourt and his Huguenot associates who withdrew from the enterprise rather than transport the priests. A devout laywoman, Mme. Pons de Guercheville, then provided funds for the Jesuits. Soon, with the Queen Mother's backing, she gained control of Acadia except for Port Royal where Poutrincourt was established. This religious friction in Acadia was abruptly halted when an English expedition under Samuel Argall destroyed Port Royal.

One of the Jesuits in Acadia, the intelligent Pierre Biard, published an indispensable *Relation de la Nouvelle France* (Lyon, 1616) [32]. He urged the colonization of Acadia for the civilizing and christianizing of the *sauvages*. By civilizing he meant establishing a sedentary life, although he admitted that increased contact with Europeans brought devastating sickness to the aborigines. Only French colonists could teach these errant peoples the superiority of settled communities. The relatively mild Acadian climate and its abundant resources promised a good living for emigrants.

The trading post at Quebec stagnated in the years before 1626. Private trading companies under the general authority of Admiral Montmorency held the monopoly fur concession but neglected their obligation to support emigrants. According to Father Gabriel Sagard's *Histoire du Canada*

Fig. 1.10 Dedication to Richelieu from Samuel de Champlain, *Les voyages de la Nouvelle France occidentale, dicte Canada* (1632).
In his dedication, Champlain strongly urges Cardinal Richelieu to demand the retrocession of New France after four years of English occupation (1629–32) and to foster the rebuilding of the colony.

(Paris, 1636) [33], the companies even persecuted the first family to migrate, the Héberts. During these years, Champlain could not overcome the companies' resistance to sponsoring emigrants. And in any case, despite the writings of Champlain and Lescarbot, Canada had not shaken its reputation as a frozen desert. Champlain was barely able to resist company efforts to recall him in 1618. Subsequently, a new company, that of Montmorency in association with the Huguenot de Caen brothers, did little to alter the now traditional anticolonial attitudes of the fur-trade monopoly.

Champlain's majestic account of his life's work, the *Voyages de la Nouvelle France occidentale, dicte Canada* (Paris, 1632) [34], constitutes the principal source for these early decades. In the context of a year-by-year narrative, Champlain highlights the colonial potential of New France. He identifies its agricultural and natural resources and provides useful information about Amerindian cultures. Throughout the narrative, he attributes the colony's stagnation to the monopoly companies' selfish devotion to immediate profits and to the discord between Huguenots and Catholics. This interpretation, buttressed by missionary accounts hostile to the predominantly Huguenot companies, strongly influenced Cardinal Richelieu when he turned his attention to colonial development. Not surprisingly, Champlain's work is dedicated to the Cardinal.

Between 1615 and the English capture of Quebec in 1629, the Recollect (Franciscan) fathers labored in New France. Their role in the colony is discussed in the works of Father Sagard, *Le grand voyage* (Paris, 1632) [35] as well as in his previously mentioned *Histoire* [33], which contains many original documents, and in the *Etablissement de la foy dans la Nouvelle France* (Paris, 1691) [36] of Chrétien Le Clercq, which quotes from the unpublished and now-unavailable writings of early Recollect missionaries. In the context of describing his long and arduous voyage to Huronia (north of Lake Huron), Sagard appealed for the development of a strong colony without which the mission must fail. He chastised the monopoly companies for their discouragement of emigration. As with Champlain's work, the publication date of the *Grand voyage*, 1632, suggests the motivation. England had returned New France by the Treaty of Saint-Germain-en-Laye in that year and many voices urged the Cardinal to reestablish the colony.

CHAPTER II

Footholds, 1626–1664

WHEN CARDINAL RICHELIEU addressed the Assembly of Notables in 1626 as the recently named first minister (1624), he placed special emphasis on the restoration of France's naval, mercantile, and colonial power. The situation was indeed bleak in 1626. A century before, French corsairs had swarmed in the Caribbean in search of Spanish prey. Now, foreign corsairs attacked French merchant ships within sight of their home ports. As for the New World, France was excluded from Brazil, had failed to settle Guiana, held no islands in the Caribbean, and was largely absent from the previously flourishing Florida-Carolina coastal trade. To be sure, Frenchmen clung to footholds along the Acadian coast and occupied the great rock (Quebec) on the St. Lawrence, but English privateers in 1613 and later in 1629 demonstrated how vulnerable these outposts were. In sum, France had little to show for a century of energetic maritime activities. Clearly, the time had come for new initiatives.

Richelieu's colonial policy can only be understood in the context of his larger geopolitical imperatives. Most of all, he worked to destroy the Habsburg ring around France. Before that could be done, however,

the Huguenots' political independence and military power had to be curtailed. Only enhanced seapower could subdue their coastal strongholds, especially La Rochelle. A revitalized French navy could also carry the cold war with Spain to the Americas, where on the principle of "no peace beyond the line," it could become hot. Once the Treaty of Alais (1629) that stripped Huguenots of their political privileges was signed, Richelieu moved closer to open conflict with the Habsburgs.

The Cardinal believed that his initiatives of 1626 would aid French commerce and, as a "mercantilist," he assumed that prosperity immediately benefited the state through higher customs duties and excise taxes. He asserted, however, that the American trade was far less valuable than that of the Levant and held less promise even than that of Persia. The Cardinal supported colonization across the Atlantic because it was a matter of state prestige to preserve settlements already established. The islands of America could yield a little tobacco, fish, and fur, provide an abode for prisoners and vagabonds, and, in time, might serve as springboards for assaults on rich Spanish America. On the other hand, New France already had a thriving fur trade and could become a prosperous colony if enough colonists could be brought there. The Cardinal's support of New France as a purely Catholic preserve reflected the consensus of his advisors and of prominent missionaries that Huguenots were responsible for all the past ills of the colony. The policy also reflected Richelieu's need to placate increasingly powerful ultra-Catholic forces in France.

During the years 1626–1628 Richelieu concentrated on mercantile and colonial policies. He had himself named grand master of navigation, an office that superseded all previous institutional authorities. In 1626, he quietly sanctioned the formation of a company to colonize St. Christopher, one of the Lesser Antilles, in which he even invested his own money and ships. This concession did not prevent the Cardinal from chartering in 1627 two other companies with monopolies over all overseas trade! These companies, superficially imitative of the spectacular Dutch East India Company (1601) and the newly formed Dutch West India Company (1621), were granted extraordinary powers and privileges. He pressured the great nobles, state officials, and leading merchants to invest in these companies, and attempted to attract Dutch capital and personnel to them. Dutch associates were to teach their notoriously individualistic French partners the benefits of mercantile cooperation and to help them overcome the national ineptitude in maritime affairs. These new, giant companies in close cooperation with the government would enable France to bolster its mercantile power.

Strong resistance to the gigantic companies from the Parisian and Breton (Brittany) Parlements and from the ports persuaded the Cardinal to abandon them. Adopting a more pragmatic policy, he sanctioned the more modest Company of

New France (1628) with the purpose of reinvigorating New France and Acadia. This company floundered from the start. Its initial expedition fell into the hands of the English, at war with France from 1628 to 1632, and in 1629 Champlain surrendered Quebec. A change in Richelieu's policy toward the Huguenots created further difficulties for the company. After the Peace of Alais, the Cardinal turned against the ultra-Catholics who were not supportive of his long-range policy of belligerence toward their Spanish allies. In an effort to placate the alienated Huguenots, Richelieu ordered the already-weakened Company of New France to compensate the de Caen brothers for the loss of their earlier fur-trade concession.

In 1635, on the eve of war against the Habsburgs, Richelieu entrusted maritime questions to a small group of advisors headed by François Fouquet, father of the celebrated superintendent of finances, Nicholas Fouquet. The elder Fouquet reorganized the stagnant Company of St. Christopher as the Company of the Islands of America, which sponsored the colonization of Guadeloupe, Martinique, and other islands of the Lesser Antilles. The hand of Fouquet is also visible in efforts to prop up the Company of New France as well as in a company for the Africa and Guiana trade. After Fouquet's death in 1640, Richelieu relied on Nicholas Fouquet for the implementation of colonial policy.

It is no easy task to sum up Richelieu's legacy in colonial affairs. Without doubt, his centralization of maritime authority made the state an important factor. Where colonies were already established, Richelieu refused to see them abandoned although it cannot be said he did much to promote their development. Constantly pressed for money to support his political, diplomatic, and military initiatives in Europe, he could not or would not grant state funds to beleaguered colonial companies, as Colbert would later do. The outbreak of land war with the Habsburgs in 1635 necessarily shifted France's focus, energies, and financial strength away from colonial affairs. That the tiny outposts in New France and the Caribbean survived in subsequent years was primarily due to private initiatives in the colonies and in France.

The story of New France during Richelieu's ministry is one of false starts and slow growth. In 1626, about one hundred people wintered in New France. Thirty years later that number had increased to but two or three hundred. What a dramatic contrast to the burgeoning English colonies to the south! Why in an era plagued by economic misery, high taxes, and war did so few French emigrants choose Canada? Many of the traditional answers to this question seem inadequate, implausible, or irrelevant. How often has it been said that Frenchmen are just too attached to the *patrie* and to their villages and gardens? No doubt they are, just as are all other peoples. Nevertheless, about 7,000 Frenchmen emigrated to the Lesser Antilles in these years. Tens of thousands also crossed the Pyrenees after 1609 to occupy artisanal and mercantile positions left open by the expulsion of the Moriscos. With the case of the Puritans always in mind, historians have asserted that the exclusion of the Huguenots from New France after 1627 prevented the emigration of a large, disaffected population. In fact, after the Treaty of Alais, the government protected the Huguenots and calmed their fears, quite unlike Charles I and Laud's policies toward the Puritans. In any case, most Huguenots had long ago turned their backs on colonization, although not on overseas commerce, because of the sixteenth-century debacles discussed above. After the Edict of Nantes, it seemed akin to treason for Hugue-

nots to abandon the struggle in France for chimerical cities on a hill in a howling wilderness. What then explains the tortoiselike pace of emigration to Canada?

One problem certainly, as has been previously mentioned, was that New France had a negative image. The works of Lescarbot and Champlain had not significantly altered the popular view of Canada as a harsh, frigid land. Only the establishment of a prosperous colony could, over time, change long-held stereotypes. The Company of New France also had bad luck. In 1628, it used fifty percent of its pledged capital to dispatch about two hundred colonists in four ships, only to have them captured by English corsairs. This stunning loss discouraged investors, and discouragement turned to disillusionment when Champlain lowered the flag at Quebec in 1629. It was on the strong advice of Champlain, and in spite of company indifference, that Richelieu insisted on the return of Quebec in 1632. Then came the forced expenditure of eighty thousand *livres* to the de Caen brothers, mentioned above. In a state of near bankruptcy, the associates not surprisingly tried to cash in the rest of their chips, selling large blocks of land *(seigneuries)* and subleasing their monopoly of the fur trade. Despite these expedients, the company remained in dire straits, and an appeal for new funds saw thirty-one of the associates abandon their initial investment rather than throw good money after bad. No wonder that the company, always on the brink of bankruptcy, could not sponsor and support settlers or pay for propaganda campaigns to entice French emigrants.

Despite this bleak picture, it remains true that the seeds of the Francophone population of North America were planted in the 1630s. At least part of what the company could not do was accomplished by the extraordinary Jesuit effort in New France. Because the Jesuits believed that evangelical

Fig. II.I "De la guerre avec les Hiroquois" from Paul Le Jeune, *Relation de ce qui s'est passé en la Nouvelle France, es années 1640 et 1641* (1642.). The Jesuit Le Jeune recounts an important confrontation between the Iroquois and a French party led by Governor Montmagny. Annoyed by the French refusal to supply them with guns, the Iroquois launched guerrilla attacks that slowed the colony's growth for the next twenty-five years (1641–1666).

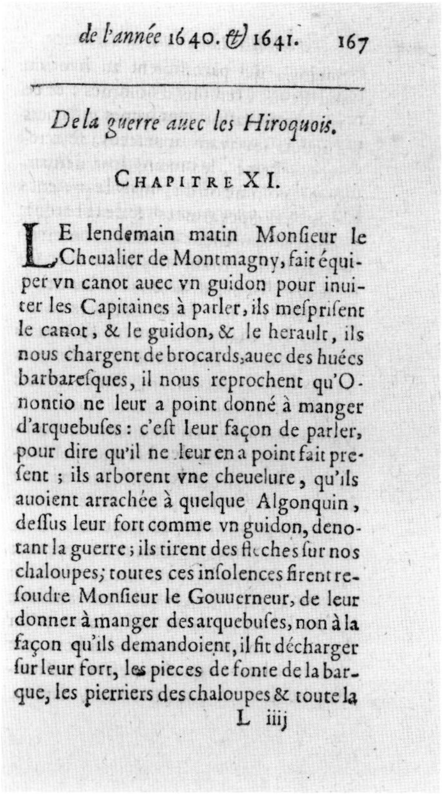

de l'année 1640. *&* 1641.   167

De la guerre auec les Hiroquois.

CHAPITRE XI.

LE lendemain matin Monſieur le Cheualier de Montmagny, fait équiper vn canot auec vn guidon pour inuiter les Capitaines à parler, ils meſpriſent le canot, & le guidon, & le herault, ils nous chargent de brocards, auec des huées barbareſques, il nous reprochent qu'Onontio ne leur a point donné à manger d'arquebuſes : c'eſt leur façon de parler, pour dire qu'il ne leur en a point fait preſent ; ils arborent vne cheuelure, qu'ils auoient arrachée à quelque Algonquin, deſſus leur fort comme vn guidon, denotant la guerre ; ils tirent des flèches ſur nos chaloupes; toutes ces inſolences firent reſoudre Monſieur le Gouuerneur, de leur donner à manger des arquebuſes, non à la façon qu'ils demandoient, il fit décharger ſur leur fort, les pieces de fonte de la barque, les pierriers des chaloupes & toute la

L iiij

activities required a colonial base to protect the missionaries from inimical *sauvages*, they generated support in France for New France. They believed that colonists would cross the Atlantic only if convinced of the prospect of a better life. But the Jesuits also assumed that if the upper classes were galvanized to support the colony and its mission, the peasant and the artisan could be induced by social pressure to emigrate. It was for these reasons that the Jesuits published their famous series of annual relations between 1632 and 1672. Even a cursory reading of these works demonstrates their effectiveness in promoting the enterprise of evangelization among an upper-class audience in the zealous grip of the Catholic revival.

Among the first and in many ways the most important Jesuit author of a *Relation* was Father Paul Le Jeune, superior of the mission at Quebec in the 1630s, and author of *Relation de ce qui s'est passé en la Nouvelle France en l'année 1633* (Paris, 1634) [37]. A converted Huguenot, Le Jeune fervently advocated the colonization of New France. He also promoted the establishment of Amerindian reserves where the *sauvages* could adapt to settled life under the Jesuits' benign tutelage. His success at inspiring support for the Canadian missions was remarkable. Under his guidance, Jérôme de La Dauversière bought the concession for Montreal in 1642. The good father persuaded the Duchesse d'Aiguillon, the niece and heir of Richelieu and for decades the principal patron of French missions around the world, to support the establishment of a hospital at Quebec.

An examination of the *Relation* of 1641 (Paris, 1642) [38] (often attributed to Father Vimont but in fact also by Le Jeune), permits an evaluation of the colony on the eve of Richelieu's death. As in the earlier work, Le Jeune discussed the desirability of domesticating *sauvages*, but he noted their fierce resistance to that idea. He also praised the spiritual work of the Duchesse and especially that of the company, despite its financial embarrassments. An ominous threat to the life of the colony appears in this relation when Le Jeune describes the fierce Iroquois attacks of 1641. Supplied with firearms by the Dutch at Albany, the Iroquois struggled to dominate the fur trade of the West and as middlemen to channel it to Albany. Le Jeune noted that he had advised Governor Montmagny to reject Iroquois peace overtures, which had called for French neutrality in the Iroquois' conflicts with France's Amerindian allies, especially the Hurons. Although this was sound advice because of New France's utter dependence on its allies for furs and security, its acceptance guaranteed the long-term Iroquoian enmity that was a major factor in stunting growth of the St. Lawrence settlements.

With far less publicity and support of Catholic zealots, Frenchmen occupied many of the Lesser Antilles during the Cardinal's ministry. This string of diminutive islands running from the Venezuelan coast north to the Greater Antilles had been bypassed by the Spaniards except as places to gather wood and water under the watchful eyes of the fiercely independent Caribs. In the first decades of the seventeenth century, when the growing popularity of tobacco meant greater demand and high prices, these islands became attractive. In 1625, a penniless French noble and corsair Pierre Belain d'Esnambuc put in at St. Christopher to repair his battered ship and there found English and French tobacco planters. He persuaded Richelieu to form the small Company of St. Christopher to settle the island. The Cardinal invested, as noted above, in the enterprise and in 1629 protected its tobacco by a tariff on foreign leaf. For the company's charter as well as for a magnificent multivolume collection of primary sources for the history of the French islands,

the reader must consult Moreau de Saint-Méry's *Loix et constitutions des colonies françoises* (Paris, 1784–[1790]) [39].

The company (1626–1635) recruited significant numbers of Norman *seigneurs* and *engagés* (indentured servants), especially when compared with the meager number lured to Canada. D'Esnambuc in 1627 recruited about five hundred *engagés* from the Havre region. Under his inspired leadership, the colony survived in a hostile environment of Caribs and English, and weathered even the dispersal of the settlement by the Spaniards in 1629, that bad year for French colonies. Even the growing indifference of company officials, almost all "volunteered" by Richelieu for state service, did not discourage the colony, which quickly tied its fortunes instead to enterprising Dutch merchants. An account of this rather murky period of the French Caribbean is fortunately available in the invaluable histories of the Dominican "Herodotus of the Indies," Father Jean Baptiste Du Tertre (*Histoire générale des isles de S. Christophe*, Paris, 1654 [40] and *Histoire générale des Antilles*, Paris, 1667–1671) [41]. He published numerous official documents and private letters, many of which are no longer extant in manuscript form.

The reorganization of the company in 1635 as the Company of the Islands of America resulted in the decision to expand to the important but dangerous islands of Martinique and Guadeloupe. Part of the danger and part of the attraction of the islands were their proximity to Spain's supply lines. The annual fleet of Spain regularly watered at Dominica, the island between Martinique and Guadeloupe. These three islands were also strongholds of the Caribs, who would bitterly oppose Frenchmen who had expelled them from St. Christopher in a sneak night attack. The Caribs were always willing to truck with passing European ships, but they had also always attacked invaders

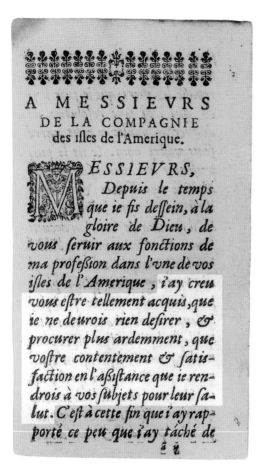

Fig. II.2 Dedication to
"Messieurs de la Compagnie"
from Jacques Bouton, *Relation
de l'éstablissement des François
depuis l'an 1635* (1640).
The first published missionary
relation of the islands was less
concerned with evangelization
of the Caribs than with promoting the interests of the
directors of the Company of
the Islands of America, to
whom this work by the Jesuit
Bouton is dedicated.

of their lands. As a result, these reputedly insatiable cannibals had acquired the most universally negative image in Europe of any Amerindian group, including the Iroquois.

Nevertheless, a seasoned colony of veterans of St. Christopher led by d'Esnambuc's nephew, Du Parquet, established itself at Martinique. With much greater difficulty and with horrendous losses, a large group of settlers from France barely held on at Guadeloupe until a truce was secured with the Caribs in 1640. Du Tertre [40] unflinchingly blamed the colonists for bringing on these difficulties by their raids on Carib gardens during the starving time.

A significant change of course for the Company of the Islands was its avid espousal of missionary work. Previously, few priests had worked at St. Christopher, but after 1635 Capuchins, Dominicans, Jesuits and some minor orders toiled in the islands. Most company directors were zealots of the Catholic revival, and François Fouquet was a particular friend and patron of the Jesuits. Cardinal Richelieu secured commitments from the Dominicans and Capuchins. The dispatch of the monks with papal authorization was not only an explicit repudiation of Spanish pretensions to monopoly but also an effective counter to French ultra-Catholic unrest about the declaration of war with Spain. The company directors enthusiastically supported these missions, and the missionaries wrote relations of their activities that served as propaganda for the company. The very first relation, entitled *Relation de l'éstablissement des François depuis l'an 1635*, by the Jesuit Jacques Bouton (Paris, 1640) [42], was dedicated to the company. These works, although unfortunately not as regularly published as the Canadian relations, make possible a deeper and more detailed view of island developments after 1640.

Colonial historians have depicted the years between Richelieu's death in 1642 and

Colbert's assumption of control in maritime affairs (1662–1663) as an era of *métropole* neglect. Operating under the regency of Anne of Austria, Richelieu's handpicked successor Cardinal Mazarin had neither the energy nor resources to pursue both land war against the Habsburgs and maritime operations. Beset by growing social and political protests in the 1640s, Mazarin barely survived the rebellion against absolute monarchy known as the Fronde (1648–

1653). Even after 1653, Mazarin focused his energies on the continuing war with Spain. In fact, to gain Oliver Cromwell's support against Spain, the Cardinal gave republican England carte blanche in the Atlantic. It is, therefore, not surprising that Mazarin took money from naval appropriations to pay army costs. No wonder, then, that naval forces declined precipitously, that French merchants became easy prey for corsairs, and that the colonies were left to their own

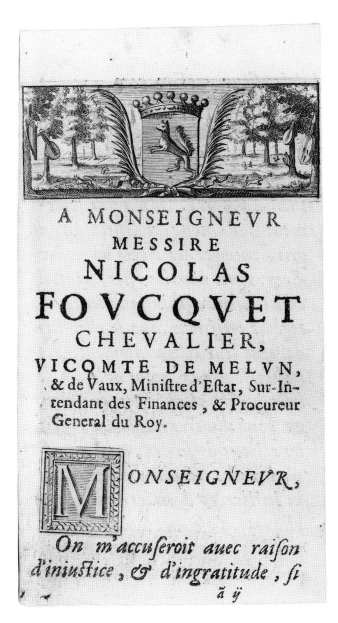

Fig. II.3 Dedication to Fouquet from Pierre Pelleprat, *Relation des missions des PP. de la Compagnie de Jésus* (1655). With this dedication the Jesuit Pelleprat hoped to interest the powerful minister Nicholas Fouquet in his colonial enterprise in Guiana. Fouquet followed in the footsteps of his father François as a great patron of the Jesuit missions.

devices. After 1647, the Company of the Islands sold its proprietary rights to governors of each island, and the Company of New France sold its fur-trade monopoly to an association of leading colonists in 1645. Although Mazarin's single-minded choice of priorities was probably crucial to his ultimate success against the Habsburgs, generations of colonial historians have had few charitable words for him.

This brief review of Mazarin's policies is, however, not the whole story. Especially after the Fronde, Mazarin and his clients attempted to strengthen French interests in Madagascar, Guiana, and Acadia. The Cardinal himself invested in companies for Madagascar and Guiana, as did his chief steward Jean-Baptiste Colbert. Some improvements in naval funds occurred during the late 1650s as the war with Spain drew to a close. But Mazarin's most significant act in maritime affairs was his selection of Nicholas Fouquet in 1655 to oversee colonial affairs.

Fouquet had continued his father's involvement in colonial affairs and when in 1653 he received the powerful office of superintendent of finances, he was positioned to make an impact. He invested in colonial and commercial companies and, like his father, took an active interest in missionary work. In the dedication to Fouquet of his *Relation des missions des PP. de la Compagnie de Jésus* (Paris, 1655) [43], the Jesuit Pierre Pelleprat lauded the superintendent's long-term devotion to the missions. Fouquet bought *seigneuries* in New France and in the Antilles, and after 1658 tried to diminish English influence in Acadia. With the winding down of the Spanish war in 1658, Fouquet moved to restore France's maritime position. He passed and enforced a tonnage tax on foreign shipping, an effort to undermine Dutch supremacy at sea. At his own expense, the superintendent fortified and expanded the facilities of Belle-Île, a strategic island off the Breton coast. According to the superintendent and his friends, Belle-Île was intended to replace Amsterdam as the entrepôt of northern Europe. In the very year of his arrest (1661), Fouquet launched a gigantic monopoly company for the East and West Indies, which was to have Belle-Île as its home base. To be sure, the ever-suspicious Colbert and King Louis XIV viewed these maritime maneuvers as merely a pretext by Fouquet to resist with force any effort to remove him from office.

Whatever his ultimate loyalties and intentions, Fouquet possessed neither the power nor the drive to return the colonies to metropolitan control and stimulate their development. Increasingly the *grand seigneur* in the 1650s, he emulated Cardinal Richelieu by delegating authority in maritime affairs to the very able Pierre Chanut, who was in effect Fouquet's "Fouquet." Chanut was to complain more than once about the superintendent's inattention to maritime affairs. Thus in 1661, although Fouquet had outlined a general plan for rebuilding the colonial empire, it would be his successor and great enemy Colbert who would implement it.

An uneven state of development best characterizes France's colonies in the Americas between the years 1642 and 1661. On the negative side, the *sauvages* of America everywhere challenged French colonies. The Iroquois pinned down the small garrison-settlements of New France, and the terror they inspired is poignantly evoked in the Jesuit relations of these years. In the Antilles, Caribs and French fought a desperate war between 1654 and 1659, and at one point Martinique survived only because of the fortuitous arrival of Dutch ships. Father Du Tertre in his *Histoire générale des Antilles* [41] depicts vividly the agonies of this struggle. The Carib-speaking Galibis of Guiana twice destroyed major colonial initiatives (1643–45, 1652–54). It must have seemed to contemporaries that some sinister force had organized this universal campaign against the French.

On the positive side, these two decades witnessed significant population growth in New France and an even greater increase in the islands. The Antilles enjoyed prosperity because of their lucrative Dutch connection. Backed by Dutch credit and technology, some island planters shifted profitably from tobacco to sugar. To sum up, despite the loss of influence in Acadia, the failures at Guiana, and Amerindian troubles everywhere, the prognosis for colonial development was not nearly as bleak as Colbert made it out to be when he came to power.

Still basking in its reputation as the gateway to El Dorado, Guiana was the goal of three major expeditions during Mazarin's ministry (1642–1661). Ever since the expulsion from Brazil, dyewood traders, tobacco growers, and would-be conquistadors cast hungry eyes on Guiana. In 1633, Richelieu granted the trade of this coast to a merchant syndicate headed by Jean Rosée, which created a tiny post at the island of Cayenne. This company granted its rights at Guiana in 1638 to the merchant Jacob Bontemps, who in return promised to transport one thousand colonists there over a thirty-year period. It was under Bontemps's aegis that a Norman nobleman Poncet de Brétigny led an ill-starred expedition of three hundred men to Guiana in 1643. According to the expedition's chronicler, Paul Boyer (*Véritable relation de tout ce qui s'est fait et passé*, Paris, 1654) [44], Brétigny and his associates were fired by dreams of quick wealth. As so often happened, Brétigny became a petty king, and his policies alienated colonists and Galibis. Sickness, food shortages, and attacks by the Galibis finished the colony. Boyer, who experienced this failure firsthand, fiercely denied that Guiana was somehow inappropriate for European settlement. He placed all of the blame on Brétigny.

The Fronde undoubtedly increased the willingness of Parisians to leave the not-so-belle France of rebellion, war, and famine. In 1651 a group of literati, which included the playwright Paul Scarron, the future Mme. de Maintenon (later the morganatic wife of Louis XIV), the poet Segrais, and the courtesan Ninon de Lenclos publicized their intent to repair to Guiana. There they would find a healthy retreat for Scarron's ailments and for the group's bleak political future given the predictable return from exile of their archenemy Mazarin. Needless to say, the plans of these would-be voyagers to Cythera came to naught, but the publicity helped prepare the way for the Company of Equinoctial France, which was able to recruit over six hundred colonists for an expedition in 1652. This company had strong connections with Catholic zealots like the Duchesse d'Aiguillon and the powerful and secretive Company of the Holy Sacrament.

The Company of Equinoctial France launched the most powerful promotional campaign of any such organization up to that time. Pamphlets were published that depicted Guiana as a terrestial paradise (*Proiet d'une compagnie* [Paris, 1651] [45]; *Mémoire pour servir de brève instruction*, Paris, 1653) [46]. A particularly interesting poster by Israel Silvestre, depicting a well-established French settlement at Cayenne, the *Descente faite par les François en la terre ferme de l'Amérique* [Paris, 1653] [47], promised free passage and free food until the colonist was on his feet. Boyer's *Véritable relation* [44] was sponsored by the company, as was the book of Jean de Laon d'Aigremont who returned to France for reenforcements in 1653. D'Aigremont's *Relation du voyage des François* (Paris, 1654) [48] discussed the first months of the colony. One piece of evidence suggesting a Mazarin connection with the company is Boyer's dedication of his book [44] to Jean Baptiste Colbert, the custodian of the Cardinal's funds.

This propaganda effort only made the

L'ISLE de Cayenne dont on voit icy le Port, & le Fort que les François de la Compagnie de l'Amerique y ont fait de
est encore plus grande que celle de paſſer à ſainct Chriſtophle & aux autres Iſles voiſines, les vaiſſeaux de la Compagni
iuſques à tant que leur trauail & la terre qu'ils cultiuent leur produiſe dequoy payer leur paſſage & leur ſubſiſtance : il par
les vaiſſeaux de la Compagnie (ſans parler des vaiſſeaux eſtrangers) iront & viendront auec vn profit & vne commodité
de faire voir icy l'ordre que les François ont tenu à y prendre terre, afin que l'on puiſſe iuger par là, que la Compagnie e

A La Mer.   ORDRE ALPHABETIQVE POVR I

B La Terre Ferme peuplée de quantité d'Indiens fertile en toutes choſes par la temperie de l'Air & du Printemps, qui y re
l'année, n'y ayant iamais ny de trop exceſſiues chaleurs, ny d'hyuer, à cauſe de l'égalité des iours & des nuicts.

C Le coſté de l'Iſle de Cayenne où eſt le Port, & qui s'eſtend le long du riuage de la Mer, vers l'endroit où l'on a fait la de
pied de la montagne nommée Ceperoux, cette Iſle de Cayenne a enuiron quarante lieuës de tour.

D Le Port capable de contenir 4000. vaiſſeaux eſt joignant l'emboucheure de la riuiere de Cayenne, qui donne ſon nom
E Riuiere de Cayenne large de huict à neuf cens pas, qui ſe ſepare en deux branches, dont elle enuironne l'Iſle aux deux c
de laquelle elle fait deux emboucheures conſiderables, apres auoir conſerué ſa largeur & ſon courant prés de deux c
auant dans la Terre Ferme.

F Deux grands vaiſſeaux qui porterent les 800. François dans le Pays l'vn nommé la Charité, l'autre S. Pierre, du port
à cinq cens tonneaux chacun, l'vn armé de 32. pieces de Canon, & l'autre de 36.

G Vne fregate de 50. tonneaux, & deux autres barques qui eſtoient en fagot dans les grands vaiſſeaux que l'on monta
l'arriuée dans le pays.

AVEC L

contredit la plus delicieuſe à habiter de toutes les Iſles de l'Amerique, & la plus lucratiue à cultiuer; La facilité d'y paſſer
item̃ent vn milier peſant à chaque paſſager, on y paſſe de meſme ceux qui n'ont point d'argent, & on leur fournit des viures
t du mois de Nouembre vne flote de la riuiere de Nantes: il en partira deux mois apres vne autre. & ainſi de temps en temps
Habitans de l'Amerique que de leurs correſpondans en France: le temps aprendra le reſte, cependant on a iugé à propos
vn pareil, tant dans les affaires de la Religion, Iuſtice & Police, que dans celle de la guerre.

IGENCE DV PLAN CY-DESSVS.

Chaloupes qui ſeruirent au debarquement.

trois corps d'armée mis en bataille par ordre d'auantgarde, Corps d'armée & arriere-garde en ſuite du débarquement.

retranchemens du camp.

e Camp où tous les eſquipages furent deſchargez.

a Montagne de Ceperoux, où fut conſtruit le Fort compoſé de cinq baſtions ſi auantageuſement ſitué, qu'il commande
oucheure de la riuiere, toute l'eſtenduë du Port & la Mer, l'on y mit d'abord 20. pieces de canon pour ſa deffence.

Indiens qui vinrent ſaluër nos François, & les preſens qu'ils ſe firent reciproquement.

eux Canots ou Chaloupes des Indiens qui furent à bord de nos vaiſſeaux pour en admirer la grandeur.

lieu où fut planté la Croix.

tes defftrichées où les viures furent plantez, en ſuite dequoy chacun trauailla à ſon habitation particuliere, & on com-
ca à planter les cannes à ſucre, & toutes les autres marchandiſes qui croiſſent dans le pays, dont on fait la recolte quatre
l'année.

EGE DV ROY.

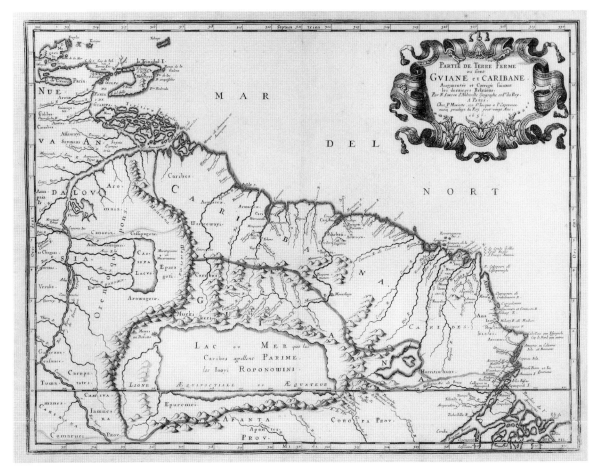

PRECEDING PAGE:
Fig. II.4 "Descente faite par les François" from Israel Silvestre, *La descente faite par les François en la terre ferme de l'Amérique* (1653). (Print).
A poster depicting the landing of the French expedition of 1652 at Cayenne (Guiana). This propaganda piece describes Cayenne as the "most delicious" of the islands and promises that the company will provide free passage for emigrants and assistance for them once arrived.

Fig. II.5 Map of "Guiane et Caribane" by Sanson (1656). This map of northern South America, probably published to elicit support for Pelleprat's expedition of 1656, highlights "Lac Parime" on whose shores lies the city of Manoa, home of El Dorado. Guiana's rivers would provide passage for discoverers of this mythical golden city.

subsequent failure of the expedition more disastrous. If not so tragic, the expedition's deterioration would be comic. On board ship, the chief company associates murdered the commander Roiville because he showed signs of becoming another Brétigny. At Cayenne, disease, food shortages, and troubles with the Galibis led to the death or dispersal of the colonists. Among the survivors was the Abbé Antoine Biet who in his *Voyage de la France équinoxiale en l'isle de Cayenne* (Paris, 1664) [49] blamed the colony's failure on poor leadership and the inexperience of the settlers. Like Boyer, Biet praised Cayenne highly as a potential colonial site.

Despite the disillusionment fostered by this second debacle, another company sponsored two expeditions in 1656–57. Father Pelleprat, a missionary at Guiana, persuaded a group of Parisians to form the Company of Meridional America. Pelleprat's previously noted *Relation* [43] vaunted Guiana's superiority to the tiny Lesser Antilles. His promotion of a Guiana colony attracted the usual Catholic zealots but also Anne of Austria and Nicholas Fouquet, to whom Pelleprat dedicated his book. The energetic company published promotional pamphlets and dispatched a reconnaissance voyage to establish a fort at the Ouatinigo River (the Dutch having occupied Cayenne since 1654). The expedition leader sent an optimistic report to Paris, and the company quickly shipped 150 colonists, including Bertrand d'Ogeron of later fame at Saint Domingue. Arrived at Martinique, the colonists found to their dismay that the leader of the first expedition had abandoned Ouatinigo and appropriated company supplies to establish a sugar plantation at Martinique. The would-be settlers either returned to France, stayed at Martinique, or, like d'Ogeron went raiding in the Caribbean. Father Du Tertre [41] is the unique printed primary source for this colony's history.

There is some evidence that among this company's backers were Cardinal Mazarin and Nicholas Fouquet. Could these expeditions have been the first stage in a projected assault on the Spanish Empire? Both expeditions were composed solely of heavily armed *men*, which was not true of the 1652 enterprise. Also in 1655, the Comte de Pagan dedicated to Mazarin his *Relation historique et géographique* (Paris, 1655) [50], a translation of Spanish works on the Amazon. Pagan appealed to the Cardinal for the creation of an equatorial French empire with Peru, the Amazon, and Guiana as borders. Finally, Fouquet noted in his memoirs that serious discussions of colonial affairs with Mazarin occurred in 1655. This conjuncture of facts provides circumstantial evidence that the Company of Meridional America's expeditions were part of a French "Western Design."

If these three major expeditions to Guiana suggest a strong French preference for warm-weather colonies, then the flow of emigrants to the islands in these years confirms the proposition. In 1645, there were roughly 8,500 French in the Caribbean as compared with some 300 in New France. Even the tobacco glut of the 1640s apparently did little to slow emigration, for one of the peak periods of *engagé* contracts at La Rochelle occurred between 1642 and 1647. During the difficult Fronde years, the islands had strong connections with the Dutch and probably achieved both economic and demographic growth.

There were many reasons why the French found the islands attractive. Impoverished Breton and Norman nobles found the lure of the Caribbean enticing with its double promise of plantations and piracy. In turn, these nobles brought indentured servants from their home areas. The island governors' toleration of Huguenots made settlement by these dissenters possible. Although they undoubtedly exaggerated, the Catholic missionary authors loudly complained about the large numbers of "heretics" in the Caribbean. Finally, although impossible to measure to what degree, an organized promotional campaign probably had some success in counteracting stereotypes of the islands as cannibal-infested jungles where disease and grotesque insects hounded settlers. Often these writers were indebted to the Company of the Islands, the proprietary governors after 1647, or government ministers.

Missionary authors asserted that colonization was necessary to create a base from which to proselytize the Amerindians, and therefore their works promoted the islands as attractive homes for French emigrants. Bouton's *Relation* (1640) [**42**] strove to "disabuse those who cannot believe that there are so many good things in those islands." He and later missionaries like Pacifique, de Provins (*Briève relation du voyages des isles de l'Amérique*, Paris, 1646) [**51**], Maurile de Saint Michel (*Voyage des isles Camercanes*, Le Mans, 1652) [**52**], and Father Du Tertre [**40, 41**] employed a strategy of realism. They did not deny that there were inconveniences in the islands—no wheat or grapes would grow there, for example; the heat was occasionally oppressive, and the Caribs were sometimes hostile. These annoyances were minor, however, compared with the wealth that hardworking planters made there and were offset by the civility and generosity of the colonists.

Special note should be taken of the missionaries' efforts to destroy the negative stereotypes of the Caribs. If these native people were viewed as irredeemably evil, how could they be candidates for conversion and civilization? Father Raymond Breton, a Dominican who worked and lived with the Caribs on the island of Dominica as a solitary missionary, testified in his man-

uscript writings to the basic humanity of his charges. Every subsequent Dominican author used Breton's firsthand observations. Most notable was Father Du Tertre [**40, 41**], who went the farthest in efforts to rehabilitate the reputation of the Caribs. Du Tertre viewed them as the "most content, the happiest, the least vicious, the most sociable, the least artificial, and the least tormented with sickness of all the nations of this world." He and his fellow Dominicans, in the tradition of their Spanish brother Las Casas, often blamed the French for the wars of the period. Pelleprat [**43**] asserted that the Caribs "had a better spirit, were more docile" than African slaves and "had as much spirit as our peasants," all of which was far removed from the unmitigated condemnations of the past. It is thanks to these missionaries that significant ethnographical and linguistic materials have survived concerning these all-but-extinct peoples.

Among secular authors of this era, by far the most important was Charles de Rochefort, whose *Histoire naturelle et morale des îles Antilles de l'Amérique* (Rotterdam, 1658) [**53**] benefited from information provided by the island governors, notably Poincy of St. Christopher and Houel of Guadeloupe. No doubt the governors provided favors to the author, who painted a charming, almost idyllic, picture of island life as well-ordered, prosperous, and cultured. Paternalistic planters, in Rochefort's view, exercised a benevolent oversight of their *engagés* and slaves. As for the Caribs, they loved the French (Rochefort's stay in the islands ended before the resumption of war in 1654). In their natural state, that is when not corrupted by the devil, Spaniards, or Englishmen, the Caribs were "civil, courteous, reasonable, docile, honest, amiable, and generous."

It is impossible to gauge the impact of these propagandists on French images and *a*

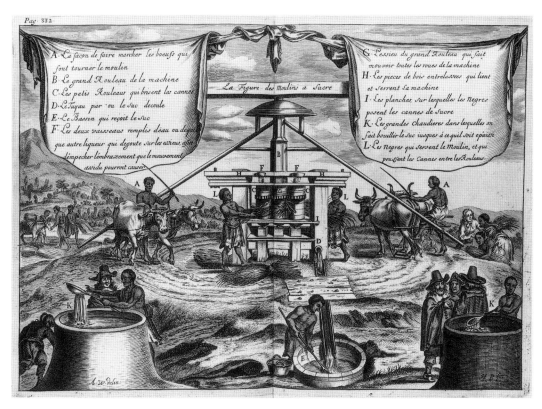

Fig. 11.6 "Moulins à sucre" from Charles de Rochefort, *Histoire naturelle et morale des îles Antilles de l'Amérique* (1665). Introduced into the French islands in the 1640s, probably by Jewish refugees from war-torn Brazil, the sugar "engine" transformed island life. The slaves feeding cane to the rollers often lost hands and arms.

fortiori to establish a causal connection between images and emigration. All that can be stated is that as greater and greater numbers of French settled in the islands, literary sources combating traditional views became widely available to the literate public.

These books provide at least an impressionistic picture of island life before the Colbert era. It is apparent that frontier conditions in combination with the prevalent colonial psychology of grasping for quick wealth broke down many of the social restraints that checked aggressive behavior at home. More readily than in New France, the islands provided opportunities to exploit fellow humans for quick dividends. It is probably germane, too, that clerical influence was less prevalent in the Antilles. Already by the 1640s, the *engagé* system had degenerated from one based on close bonds between master and servant to a more impersonal, exploitative institution. Ship captains developed the trade into a lucrative business, and, according to Pelleprat [43], many *engagés* were tricked into signing contracts or were even kidnapped. Authors like Maurile de Saint Michel [52] and the Abbé Biet [49] described the *engagé*'s life as one of unmitigated horror for the three years of servitude.

Relatively little material in these accounts addresses the conditions of the growing numbers of black slaves, but as servants for life they were possibly treated better than the *engagés*. Some writers considered Africans as gross and stupid as animals. Father Du Tertre [41], who devoted hundreds of pages to the Caribs, provided less information about Africans. He did say that owners treated blacks like horses but that the slaves did not seem to mind as long as they had food. Although he viewed Africans as naturally stupid and ignorant, he applauded the constancy of those converted to Christianity. Pelleprat [43], who described blacks as dumb and hideous, reasserted the traditional argument that slavery was the prerequisite for their salvation. An occasional document concerning the treatment of slaves can be found in Moreau de Saint-Méry's *Loix et constitutions* [39]. An edict of 1648 at Martinique, for example, enjoined planters to grow food for their slaves. Further promoting social instability in these years was the shortage of European females, which inevitably encouraged concubinage and increased the attractiveness of the buccaneering life. In short, the islands were very fortunate to have had strong, long-lived, and just governors (Poincy, Houel, and Du Parquet) who ensured at least some measure of social and political cohesion.

The history of New France in these two decades has a number of similarities to that of the Antilles: a decline of centralized authority, collapse of the proprietary company, and rising population. In the same year (1645) that Poincy's revolt against the Company of the Islands led to its bankruptcy, the Company of New France sold its fur-trade monopoly to the Company of the Habitants, an association of leading colonists. The great Jesuit effort in New France, as well as that of private Catholic associations, surpassed that in the islands. Unlike island missionaries who often found themselves in opposition to the governors, the Jesuits in New France played an important role in the colonial government. Population growth in these decades, although not as dramatic as in the Antilles, was significant. The increase from some three hundred to perhaps three thousand in 1662 occurred independently of state initiatives.

After 1640, when the Company of New France sold concessions to a variety of sublesees, the Society of Notre Dame bought the island of Montreal. Led by La Dauversière, it created a settlement that struggled heroically against repeated Iroquois assaults and guerrilla tactics. Only fifty colonists remained in 1652 ten years after establishment. Thanks to valiant efforts of the society, *dévot* groups in France rallied to Montreal's cause. In 1653, a recruitment of 110 colonists saved beleaguered Montreal. It was the Jesuits along with the new bishop Laval who persuaded Louis XIV in 1659 to dispatch aid and men against renewed Iroquois attacks. Montreal and New France survived this terrible decade.

A principal historical source for this era of New France, as for the previous decades, is the collection of reports known as Jesuit relations, all available at the John Carter Brown Library. They echo the earlier relations in their advocacy of colonization. Most Jesuit authors presented a favorable picture of France's Amerindian allies, especially the Hurons. But these relations also contained annual accounts of the key events. Father Vimont's *Relation de ce qui s'est passé en la Nouvelle France* of the events of 1642–43 (Paris, 1644) [54] made plain the Iroquois threat, especially to the sedentary Huron communities. He pleaded for patrons in France to support and protect those "gentle lambs" against the "wolfish" Iroquois. In his *Relation de ce qui s'est passé de plus remarquable* of 1650–51 (Paris, 1652) [55], Paul Ragueneau sadly described the devastating Iroquois attacks on Huronia and the perilous situation at Montreal. It also clearly exposed the negative consequences of the Iroquois wars on the colony's fur trade, at this time dependent on Amerindian middlemen voyaging to Montreal and Quebec. After a brief truce in the middle 1650s, New France once more had to bear the horrors of Iroquois war. But then in 1659 the king, relieved of the expense of the Spanish conflict, demonstrated a willingness to help. Jérôme Lallemant's *Relation de ce qui s'est passé de plus remarquable* of 1659 and 1660 (Paris, 1661) [56] and Le Jeune's of 1660 and 1661 (Paris, 1662) [57] both made a strong appeal for enough French soldiers to render possible a frontal assault on Iroquois villages.

In 1662, the people of New France brought the issue directly to Louis XIV's court. The governor Du Bois d'Avaugour dispatched the commander of Trois-Rivières, Pierre Boucher, to Paris where he made a favorable impression on the young king. Boucher subsequently wrote a short, straightforward account of the colony (*Histoire véritable et naturelle*, Paris, 1664) [58] to inform France and the man to whom it was dedicated, Jean-Baptiste Colbert. In the same year, 1662, Laval undertook the crossing to add his potent voice to the clamor for aid, as well as to campaign successfully for the governor's recall. Strong momentum for royal intervention was in progress, and young Louis appeared personally touched by accounts of heroic Frenchmen struggling for security in a wintry wilderness. The very next spring would see the termination of the Company of New France and the dispatch of royal officials to investigate conditions.

Louis and Colbert also had to face the problem of English encroachment in Acadia and Newfoundland. The Cromwell regime and private corsairs had been extremely effective in the 1650s, resulting in the near elimination of French influence in these commercially and strategically important regions. Fouquet had attempted to deal with the declining French influence by sending Nicholas Gargot as governor to Placentia, Newfoundland. This intervention by the powerful superintendent drew hot protests from fishermen who, along with many subsequent historians, believed that Fouquet meant to extract payment for protection against England. Gargot's mission came to naught because of Fouquet's arrest. In 1663, therefore, English influence still predominated in Acadia and Newfoundland.

pardevers eux, et la dame Houel et ledit sieur de Cérillac, qui sont présentement en cette Ville de Paris, seront tenus de satisfaire dans ledit temps, du jour de la signification qui leur sera faite du présent Arrêt. FAIT au Conseil d'Etat du Roi, Sa Majesté y étant, tenu à Paris, le dix-septieme Avril mil six cent soixante-quatre.

Signé DE LYONNE.

EDIT portant Etablissement d'une Compagnie des Indes Occidentales, pour faire tout le Commerce dans les Isles et Terre ferme de l'Amérique, et autres Pays, aux concessions, pouvoirs, facultés, droits, exemptions et Privileges y contenus, et Arrêts du Parlement et de la Chambre des Comptes de Paris sur icelui.

Des 28 Mai, 11 et 31 Juillet 1664.

LOUIS, etc. SALUT. La paix dont jouit présentement cet Etat, nous ayant donné lieu de nous appliquer au rétablissement du Commerce, nous avons reconnu que celui des Colonies et de la Navigation sont les seuls et véritables moyens de le mettre dans l'éclat où il est chez les Etrangers; pour à quoi parvenir et exciter nos Sujets à former de puissantes Compagnies, nous leur avons promis de si grands avantages, qu'il y a lieu d'espérer que tous ceux qui prendront quelque part à la gloire de l'Etat, et qui voudront acquérir du bien par les voies honorables et légitimes y entreront très-volontiers; ce que nous avons déjà reconnu avec beaucoup de joie par la Compagnie qui s'est formée depuis quelques mois pour la Terre ferme de l'Amérique, autrement appellée *France Equinoxiale*; mais comme il ne suffit pas à ces Compagnies de se mettre en possession des Terres que nous leur concédons, et les faire défricher et cultiver par les gens qu'ils y envoient avec grand frais, si elles ne se mettent en état d'y établir le Commerce, par le moyen duquel les François qui s'habitueront auxdits Pays, communiquent avec les naturels Habitans, en leur donnant en échange des denrées qui croissent dans leurs Pays, les choses dont ils ont besoin, il est aussi absolument nécessaire pour faire ce Commerce, d'équiper nombre de Vaisseaux pour porter journellement les marchandises qui se débitent audit Pays, et rapporter en France celles qui s'en retirent, ce qui n'a point été fait jusqu'à présent par les Compagnies ci-devant formées; ayant reconnu que le Pays de Canada a été abandonné par les Intéressés en la

Fig. III.1 "Loix et constitutions" from Moreau de Saint-Méry, *Loix et constitutions des colonies françoises* (1784–1790). Copy of the edict establishing Colbert's West India Company in 1664. In the preamble, Louis XIV explains the need for a powerful, state-supported company to exploit the trade of Africa and the Americas. The company lasted until 1674.

CHAPTER III

The Establishment of the Old Colonial System, 1664–1688

HE ACCESSION OF a young and energetic Louis XIV to power in 1661 combined with Mazarin's achievement of peace created the potential for significant maritime renewal. Among Louis' first measures was the appointment of a council of commerce, headed by Fouquet and including Jean-Baptiste Colbert. Its call for advice yielded seven volumes of memoranda and reports. However, the dramatic arrest of Fouquet aborted that initiative, and two years passed before Colbert could implement plans to assert royal authority in the colonies and promote their development.

Was Colbert, the man generally praised as the shaper of the first colonial empire, prepared to oversee maritime affairs? In some respects, he was. As trustee of Mazarin's household and fortune, Colbert had been responsible for the Cardinal's investments in commercial companies, and archival sources give early evidence of his famous thirst for information. Colbert quite likely invested in one and possibly two of the Guiana companies. He knew enough to write intelligent memoirs to the Cardinal about the need to revive France's sea power and commerce. Further evidence of his knowl-

edge of these matters was his appointment to the Council of Commerce of 1661.

On the other hand, Colbert had few contacts with naval and colonial personnel. Because Fouquet had organized a widespread clientage in the navy, his arrest left Colbert with a perplexing problem. Out of sheer necessity, Colbert had to ignore the offenses of those Fouquet clients who were, often with alacrity, willing to switch loyalties. Colbert's initial lack of experienced, trusted advisors and his ignorance of conditions in the colonies led to false steps and setbacks, for example, Laval's successful campaign to oust Du Bois d'Avaugour and replace him with a personal friend. When Colbert's later policy of close supervision of ecclesiastical authority is recalled, his concurrence with Laval is startling. Furthermore, Laval was closely identified with the *dévot* party, which by 1662 was supporting the incarcerated Fouquet. Correspondence in 1662 and 1663 between Colbert and the Comte d'Estrades, the new viceroy of America, was filled with laments about their ignorance of the situation in the islands. D'Estrades complained that a new governor for the buccaneer island of Tortuga had been appointed without his consent and Colbert, only later minister of the marine (1669), had to admit he knew nothing about the matter. Neither man knew the appointee, Bertrand d'Ogeron.

Colbert's personnel decisions in these years left much to be desired. Take the case of Nicholas Le Febvre de La Barre. Although he was such a poor intendant in the 1650s that Colbert himself had complained to Mazarin, La Barre was entrusted in 1663 with the formation of the Company for Guiana, which was the keystone of Colbert's plans for the colonies. Further complaints about La Barre ensued, in particular a caustic one from Colbert de Terron, Colbert's cousin and chief advisor for maritime questions. Nevertheless, the minister gave a long series of commands to La Barre. At one point, Colbert explained his choice of La Barre by complaining of the difficulty of finding intelligent men for overseas posts. Fortunately for Colbert, poverty pushed two very distinguished men to accept colonial positions. Colbert inherited d'Ogeron, who had failed to find fortune in the Caribbean, as governor of Saint Domingue. As for Alexander Prouville de Tracy, the great commander of the 1664 expedition to restore royal authority in the American colonies, debts brought this sexagenarian to Colbert's doorstep in search of a position.

Louis's and Colbert's plan for establishment of royal control evolved partly from actual colonial conditions and partly from long-established official principles. Colonists in New France begged for action. At Guiana, after so much cost in money and lives, Cayenne was under Dutch control. The islands were in the hands of private proprietors who sent their exports to the Netherlands. This infuriated the "mercantilist" Colbert who urged the king to regain control of colonial commerce. In this thinking, Colbert explicitly followed Richelieu and implicitly Fouquet, whose papers Colbert thoroughly studied. Colbert chose to establish in 1664 giant companies for the West and East Indies that resembled Fouquet's aborted company of 1661.

The West India Company's (w.i.c.) first goal was the colonization of Guiana; indeed, the w.i.c. was simply the enlargement of the Company of Guiana (1663), whose mission was the capture of Cayenne. This emphasis on the development of Guiana as a supplier of the Antilles consumed the w.i.c.'s capital, and the subsequent English capture of Cayenne during the 1666–67 war crippled its finances. Another problem with Colbert's all-embracing principle of company organization was the inclusion of New France, a colony of little interest to the w.i.c.'s directors. Even Jean Talon, Colbert's great intendant at Quebec, protested. Finally, the company's installation in the islands provoked serious resistance that governors like Clodoré at Martinique and d'Ogeron at Saint Dominigue controlled only with great difficulty. In short, Colbert's assignment of colonies in greatly varied states of development to one company represented the triumph of theory over reality.

Despite these defects in personnel and design, it must be admitted that Colbert's drive and irresistible energy yielded some positive results overseas. France, he repeatedly affirmed, could profit only from prosperous colonies. Good government and good order were the prerequisites of colonial economic development. To foster these goals, Colbert exerted close supervision over colonial officials, and his orders were obeyed except when they ran directly counter to the colonies' vital interests. The colonial governors and intendants were advised not to be as harsh as would be appropriate at home, because the colonists had after all given up the delights of France. Royal officers were not to bother Huguenots and Jews or allow them to be persecuted. They were always to maintain peaceful relations with the aborigines. Only when the colonists became fat and content would large numbers of French migrate to these distant lands. To his credit, Colbert refused to consider the use of forced emigration (*forçats*), although after his death his son and successor as minister of marine, Seignelay (1683–1690), could not prevent the transportation of Huguenots.

Colbert's attitudes toward emigration were ambivalent. During the first decade (1661–1672), he strongly encouraged it. One thinks of the soldiers offered bonuses to stay after a tour of duty or of the orphan girls supplied with a trousseau who were expected to marry immediately after disembarkation at Quebec or Fort-de-France (Martinique). In this decade, the population of Saint Domingue tripled and that of New France doubled. Nevertheless, Colbert lived at a time when, in contrast to the early seventeenth century, a consensus was emerging that colonies drained needed manpower from the homeland. Colbert wanted to establish a basic breeding stock and then encourage rapid natural growth by providing subsidies to large families, by encouraging French-Indian marriages, by lowering taxes, and by preventing creditors from ruining indebted colonists.

Colbert assumed that promotional literature could aid colonial development, and numbers of books supportive of French endeavors in the East and West Indies appeared between 1664 and 1672. A common theme of these writings reflected the minister's well-known "realism" about colonial development. He often articulated his belief that colonial growth required long-term hard work and patience. Chimeras about quick riches had doomed previous efforts in Guiana and elsewhere. Painful sacrifices were the unavoidable fate of early stages of colony building. Only hardworking peasants and artisans, not useless adventurers, could hew settlements out of the wilderness. Benign conduct toward the aborigines, not flagrant violation, would permit colonial growth. An early example of this literature is Boucher's *Histoire* [58], which listed the chief disadvantages of the colony (the Iroquois, the long winters, and the mosquitoes). He added that "people of condition" were not appropriate for this still-primitive land.

The 1664 expedition to Guiana undoubtedly stimulated the publication of two major works. First was the Abbé Biet's *Voyage...en l'isle de Cayenne* [49], an analysis of the weaknesses of the 1652 colony. Within the context of blaming the expedition's leadership and the colonists' unpreparedness, Biet asserted emphatically that Guianan soil and climate were appropriate for European settlers. But potential colonists should no longer be deluded by false promises of a terrestrial paradise; only gritty labor and stoic determination would guarantee success. If he exposed many of the problems and annoyances of Guiana, it was not to "discourage those whom God inspires to emigrate to these lands." Biet listed in great detail the essentials that colonists should carry to make life there pleasant. Throughout the book, the author insisted upon a policy of just conduct toward the Galibis.

More certainly inspired by Colbert was Le Febvre de La Barre's *Description de la France équinoctiale* (Paris, 1666) [59], published after his return from Guiana. Like Biet, he blamed brutal and incompetent leaders for France's previous failures there. La Barre ignored the El Dorado myth and insisted on the necessity of well-prepared and hardworking settlers. He promoted kind treatment of the Galibis, who could supply the colony with its basic necessities as well as trade goods. For these authors, as for Colbert, only candor could overcome the

Fig. III.2 "L'Isle de Cayenne"
from Antoine Joseph Le Febvre
de La Barre, *Description de la
France équinoctiale* (1666).
After his expedition of 1664
recaptured Cayenne from the
Dutch, La Barre included this
up-to-date map in his propaganda account. The French
long claimed all of the coast
from the Amazon (top, left)
to the Maroni River (bottom,
right).

disillusionment caused by earlier, highly publicized failures.

Father Du Tertre's magnificent *Histoire générale des Antilles* [41] fitted well into this pattern of realistic colonial propaganda. The Dominican, who had had close connections with Richelieu and Nicholas Fouquet, quite evidently had access to official papers under Colbert's control. His account of early stages of Antillean development did not hide the terrible problems besetting early French settlers. However, he insisted that the islands had achieved remarkable prosperity within two decades. Indeed, with the Caribs tamed, plantations built, and the settlers' licentiousness controlled by missionary efforts, island life had become "very peaceful and very agreeable." Despite all the initial miseries he had so amply documented, Du Tertre claimed to "have never seen a man or a woman who came home who did not express a strong desire to return there."

Beyond this literary propaganda, Colbert and the w.i.c. employed every means to attract investors and colonists. Leaflets and public notices were placed in appropriate towns and villages, and bishops and priests were pressured to use their pulpits to encourage participation. Although the success of these initiatives cannot be demonstrated quantitatively, there can be no question that before 1672 Colbert mounted a strenuous campaign to create a more positive image of life in the Americas. With the start of the Dutch War (1672–78), however, the funds for such efforts were sacrificed to the voracious appetites of Louis's armies. The promotion of emigration to the colonies swiftly dried up.

The colonization of Guiana was one of Colbert's greatest goals and also one of his greatest disappointments. Almost certainly involved in previous enterprises for the "Wild Coast," the de facto colonial minister had great hope for the 1664 expedition that

evicted the Dutch from Cayenne. Success there, he assumed, would help France eliminate Dutch traders from the Antilles. Wood, cattle, and provisions from Guiana would complement plantation colonies in the French islands. Disaster, however, struck the colony three years later when an English fleet ravaged Cayenne and burnt adjacent plantations. Disappointment followed disappointment, but the tenacious Colbert refused to be discouraged and even ordered a powerful naval operation to retake Cayenne after its fall to the Dutch in 1676. At Colbert's death, Guiana would remain a French colony, albeit struggling and stagnant.

Although the colonists at Cayenne suffered from disease, the major problems of the settlement were economic, political, and psychological. After all, the Dutch next door at present-day Suriname, and in the past (1654–1664) even at Cayenne, had managed to create flourishing colonies despite problems from disease and the tropical climate. Undeveloped French Cayenne, however, could never attract enough slaves because slavers found far better prices in Dutch Guiana and in the Antilles. The w.i.c., usually depicted as a tool of Colbert, largely ignored Guiana, at least according to Jean Clodoré's otherwise laudatory account of the company (*Relation de ce qui s'est passé dans les isles & terre-ferme de l'Amérique*, Paris, 1671) [60]. The few and impoverished colonists twice saw foreigners occupy an exposed Cayenne. At Colbert's death, there were only some eight hundred whites, métis (half-breeds) and slaves at Cayenne, compared with about sixteen thousand at Martinique alone.

A small number of promotional tracts touted Guiana after 1672. A "Relation de la Guiane," perhaps written by Le Febvre de La Barre, appeared in Henri Justel's *Recueil de divers voyages faits en Afrique et en l'Amérique* (Paris, 1674) [61]; and a paraphrasing of this work was included later in Gomberville's translation of Cristóbal de Acuña's *Relation de la rivière des Amazones* (Paris, 1682) [**62**]. Also published in the Justel volume [**61**] was the letter of Fathers Grillet and Béchameil describing their amazing travels to the interior of Guiana.

As noted above, the weaning of the French Antilles from Dutch dependency was a crucial goal of Colbert. In 1664, he moved quickly against the island proprietors and sent Prouville de Tracy to bring these colonies under royal control. Tracy's series of edicts regulating island life can be found in Moreau de Saint-Méry's *Loix et constitutions* [**39**]. But even the tough Tracy could not implement Colbert's order to exclude the Dutch. The islands suffered because the w.i.c. did not have the capacity to send even fifty percent of the supplies the Dutch had. The subsequent rebellions of 1665 against the company, which were put down only after a desperate struggle, are described fully in Du Tertre's work [**41**].

Ironically, the war of 1666–67 against England forced the w.i.c. to allow France's ally, the Dutch, as well as French private traders to participate in the island trade. Colbert reimposed the restrictions against foreigners in 1668 after the war, but this exclusion was made more tolerable because of an edict of 1669 granting permission to all French ships to trade there. Colbert's correspondence with his officials, especially with the crusty Governor-General de Baas (1667–1677), suggests that his anti-Dutch measures were not always obeyed. Frustrated in their overt rebellion against the w.i.c.'s monopoly, colonists used smuggling and nonpayment of debts as indirect modes of resistance. Especially difficult were the wild frontiersmen of Saint Domingue, whose revolt of 1670–71 against the w.i.c. forced humiliating concessions from crown and company. The endless repetition of various

prohibitions is evidence that administrative fiat from Paris drew obedience only when royal officials were willing or able to implement it, and this largely depended on the attitudes of the leading colonists.

Royal policy in these decades was rather ambivalent as to the place of the Antilles in France's strategy. On the one hand, Colbert strove to keep the islands at peace. Governors were ordered to maintain peace with the Caribs at practically any price. Island officials were admonished not to pick quarrels with their neighbors. Colbert consistently refused to allow d'Ogeron to unleash the buccaneers against Spanish possessions, for example. On the other hand, Colbert advised officials to support covertly Carib attacks against other Europeans. French diplomats stalled for years at turning over English plantations at St. Christopher after the Treaty of Breda mandated their restitution. Moreover, numbers of memoirs urged Colbert to launch an all-out assault on the Spanish empire in America.

For the administration of the islands, as well as other colonies, the king named governors for each island as well as a governor-general whose position of authority was akin to that of a Spanish viceroy. These officials were overwhelmingly military men without means, and they enjoyed an authority far beyond that of governors of home provinces. Not only were they thousands of miles from Paris, but their role as military leaders of vulnerable colonies forced Colbert to overlook significant character flaws and even hints of pecuniary corruption. De Baas, governor-general of the islands, and the Comte de Frontenac of New France are prime examples. The principal official check on the governor's use of power was the intendant, who controlled colonial finances and was responsible for internal administration. Moreover, the intendant reported directly to Colbert and thus could voice grievances against the governor. In fact, however, the intendants were far weaker than their counterparts in France, for the same reasons the governors were stronger. Finally, all the colonies had by the 1670s sovereign councils, jointly named by the governor and intendant, which exercised judicial powers and thus theoretically set limits to the governors' authority.

Other than security, the central problem facing the islands in Colbert's era was the difficult transition from tobacco to sugar, indigo, and cotton. The price decline after 1640 because of competition from the North American mainland and the poor reputation of the island leaf dictated a change. Island proprietors had in the 1640s facilitated this change by granting a three-year tax exemption to those fortunate enough to have the land, capital, or credit. Tracy continued this measure in 1665, and the following year the king lowered duties on tobacco and sugar. The government inadvertently promoted the changeover from tobacco by creating an ill-advised tobacco monopoly in France that prospered by paying the planter less and charging the smoker at home more. Saint Domingue in particular was damaged, with some planters switching to indigo while many others resumed careers as buccaneers. At the same time, royal policy made the transition more difficult by giving a monopoly of the slave trade first to the w.i.c., and then to various successor companies. Despite generous subsidies—for example, a ten *livres* bonus for every slave disembarked—these companies never achieved even half their assigned quotas. The government's decision in 1684 to outlaw previously encouraged island sugar refineries and to favor metropolitan refineries threatened the economic future of the French Antilles. The edict, however, was not universally enforced, which was just as well because it would have destroyed the production of molasses,

tafia (low-grade rum), and rum in the islands.

The gradual transition from tobacco to more capital-intensive crops led to only moderate increases of whites but a dramatic growth of African slaves. Already by 1665, French officials had to make a treaty with the *marrons* (fugitive slaves) at Martinique. For security purposes, Colbert constantly encouraged the growth of the white population by halving the term of *engagés* to eighteen months, by forcing all island-bound ships to transport two *engagés*, by advocating toleration of Jews and Huguenots, and by supporting military and female emigration. In effect, Colbert espoused a contradictory policy of encouraging the slave trade for economic reasons and the *engagé* trade for security reasons. But in truth there was little land or hope for these poor whites in the islands, except at Saint Domingue.

As the numbers of slaves increased and on the advice of island officials, Colbert prepared the Black Code, which was published in 1685 during the ministry of his son, Seignelay. The apparently humanitarian statutes requiring adequate food for slaves and protecting them from excessive violence stemmed from the minister's concern about protecting a valuable commodity from uncontrolled exploitation. The Code was somewhat less harsh in punishing crimes by Africans than earlier island edicts, which can be read in *Loix et constitutions* by Moreau de Saint-Méry [39]. The Code's penalties were levied with the view of permitting continued labor from the slave. Its interdiction of the practice of freeing old or maimed slaves was a simple effort to relieve the public treasury of the burden of supporting liberated slaves. In any case, only those articles deemed acceptable to the planter elite were consistently enforced; for example, the abolition of the practice of giving slaves a day to cultivate their food in lieu of traiter de gré à gré esdites Isles et Colonies, et de faire pendant le même temps porter de la Côte de Guinée dans notre Royaume; savoir, chacune des deux premieres années la quantité de mille marcs de poudre d'or, et celle de douze cens marcs pour chacune des années suivantes.

ART. XVI. Et pour donner moyen à ladite Compagnie de soutenir son entreprise, nous voulons que conformément à ce qui s'est pratiqué jusqu'à présent, depuis le Traité fait avec Maître Jean Oudiette le 16 Octobre 1675, il soit payé à ladite Compagnie la somme de treize livres par forme de gratification pour chacune tête de Negre de Guinée qu'elle aura porté dans nos Isles et Colonies de l'Amérique sur le prix de notre Domaine d'Occident en la maniere accoutumée, en conséquence des Certificats de l'Intendant des Isles, ou des Gouverneurs en son absence, visez par les Directeurs dudit Domaine.

ART. XVII. Et à l'égard de la Poudre d'or qu'elle rapportera des Pays de sa Concession, nous voulons aussi et ordonnons être payé à ladite Compagnie, par forme de gratification en la maniere que dessus, la somme de vingt livres pour chaque marc de Poudre d'or, en rapportant les certifications du Maître et du Garde du Bureau de la Monnoie de Paris, visez par les Directeurs du Domaine d'Occident.

ART. XVIII. Ne seront par nous accordées aucunes Lettres d'Etat, de Répi, Surséance ou Evocation aux Débiteurs de la Compagnie; et si aucunes étoient obtenues de nous ou de nos Juges, nous les avons dès à présent comme dès-lors, déclarées nulles et de nulle valeur, faisant défenses à nos Juges d'y avoir égard.

Si donnons en mandement, ect. DONNÉ à Versailles au mois de Janvier, l'an de grace, 1685, et de notre regne le quarante-deuxieme. *Signé* LOUIS. *Et plus bas*, par le Roi, COLBERT.

R. au Parlement de Paris, le 22 Janvier 1685.

───────────────────────────────

CODE NOIR OU EDIT servant de Réglement pour le Gouvernement et l'Administration de la Justice et de la Police des Isles Françoises de l'Amérique, et pour la Discipline et le Commerce des Negres et Esclaves dans ledit Pays.

Du mois de Mars 1685.

LOUIS, etc. Comme nous devons également nos soins à tous les Peuples que la Divine Providence a mis sous notre obéissance, nous avons bien voulu faire examiner, en notre présence, les Mémoires qui nous ont été envoyés par nos Officiers de nos Isles de l'Amérique, par lesquels ayant été informés du besoin qu'ils ont de notre Autorité et de notre Justice pour y maintenir la Discipline de l'Eglise Catholique, Apostolique et Romaine, et pour y regler ce qui concerne l'Etat et la ·qualité des Esclaves dans nosdites Isles ; et désirant y pourvoir et leur faire connoître qu'encore qu'ils habitent des climats infiniment éloignés de notre séjour ordinaire, nous leur sommes toujours présent, non-seulement par l'étendue de notre puissance, mais encore par la promptitude de notre application à les secourir dans leurs nécessités. A CES CAUSES, de l'avis de notre Conseil, et de notre certaine science, pleine puissance et autorité Royale, nous avons dit, statué et ordonné, disons, statuons et ordonnons, voulons et nous plaît ce qui suit.

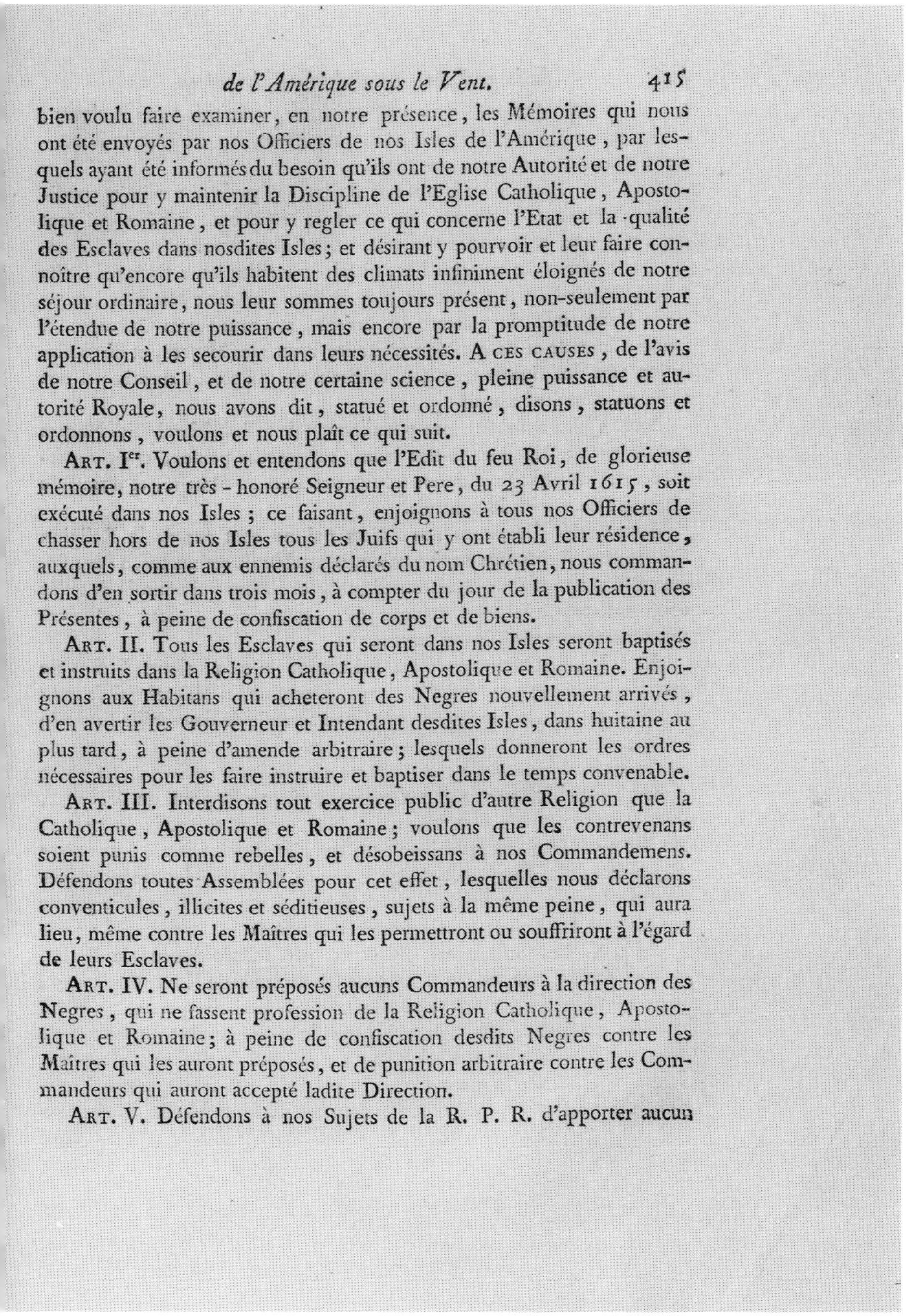

ART. Iᵉʳ. Voulons et entendons que l'Edit du feu Roi, de glorieuse mémoire, notre très - honoré Seigneur et Pere, du 23 Avril 1615, soit exécuté dans nos Isles ; ce faisant, enjoignons à tous nos Officiers de chasser hors de nos Isles tous les Juifs qui y ont établi leur résidence, auxquels, comme aux ennemis déclarés du nom Chrétien, nous commandons d'en sortir dans trois mois, à compter du jour de la publication des Présentes, à peine de confiscation de corps et de biens.

ART. II. Tous les Esclaves qui seront dans nos Isles seront baptisés et instruits dans la Religion Catholique, Apostolique et Romaine. Enjoignons aux Habitans qui acheteront des Negres nouvellement arrivés, d'en avertir les Gouverneur et Intendant desdites Isles, dans huitaine au plus tard, à peine d'amende arbitraire ; lesquels donneront les ordres nécessaires pour les faire instruire et baptiser dans le temps convenable.

ART. III. Interdisons tout exercice public d'autre Religion que la Catholique, Apostolique et Romaine ; voulons que les contrevenans soient punis comme rebelles, et désobeissans à nos Commandemens. Défendons toutes Assemblées pour cet effet, lesquelles nous déclarons conventicules, illicites et séditieuses, sujets à la même peine, qui aura lieu, même contre les Maîtres qui les permettront ou souffriront à l'égard de leurs Esclaves.

ART. IV. Ne seront préposés aucuns Commandeurs à la direction des Negres, qui ne fassent profession de la Religion Catholique, Apostolique et Romaine ; à peine de confiscation desdits Negres contre les Maîtres qui les auront préposés, et de punition arbitraire contre les Commandeurs qui auront accepté ladite Direction.

ART. V. Défendons à nos Sujets de la R. P. R. d'apporter aucun

Fig. III.3 "Code noir" from Moreau de Saint-Méry, *Loix et constitutions des colonies françoises* (1784-1790).
The famous slave code, the Code Noir, was formulated by Colbert and his son Seignelay with the principal intent of preserving slave property from over-exploitation by rapacious owners. Its relatively liberal provisions were, however, enforced only sporadically. Article I gives island Jews three months to leave, and the next articles place harsh restrictions on island Protestants.

Combat de Cayonne

Fig. III.4 "Combat de Cayonne" from Jean Baptiste Du Tertre, *Histoire générale des Antilles* (1667–1671). Depiction of a major French victory over the English colonial militia (1666) at the divided island of St. Christopher. The valor of the French colonists during this short struggle much improved their reputation in France.

giving them provisions was little enforced. In short, the French planters ruled themselves almost as autonomously as their English island neighbors, and thus the French practice of slavery was in no significant way more humane than the brutal English form. (However, a more positive view may be found in a contemporary source, Jean Clodore's *Relation*) [60]. The Black Code is reprinted in Moreau de Saint-Méry [39], and the functioning of the slave system in the late seventeenth century is described in Father Labat's popular *Nouveau voyage aux isles de l'Amérique* (Paris, 1722) [63]. Labat's perspective was that of an easygoing, paternalistic slave owner who believed that slave performance was best under a strict but just master.

During the ministry of Colbert and Seignelay, the reputation of the islands remained in a state of flux. On the one hand, the missionary relations largely ceased. Among the few such works of this period, special mention should be made of La Borde's "Relation...des Caraibes" (in Justel's *Recueil*) [61], which is a firsthand account by an embittered missionary of his unfruitful labors among the Dominica Caribs. Although that early hero Father Breton capped his career by publishing the precious *Dictionaire caraibe-françois* (Auxerre, 1665) [64], the Dominicans and other missionaries had already become pessimistic about the conversion of the Caribs. To maintain good relations with the Caribs, Colbert had to force the unwilling Jesuits to keep their religiously unproductive mission at St. Vincent. In any case, the missionary rela-

tions had apparently little impact on stereotypes of colonists as human refuse. The women sent to the islands in the 1680s were widely but unjustifiably assumed to be prostitutes and vagabonds, and the forced transport of Huguenots and galley slaves in the 1680s provided plenty of stories to fuel negative images of the colonies well into the eighteenth century.

On the other hand, the War of 1666–67 brought favorable attention to the islands at court. Literary gazettes published accounts of islander heroism in the Anglo-Dutch War (1666–67) in which France sided with the Dutch, and Father Du Tertre [41] happily recounted English defeats. Such tales of courageous colonists in battle pointedly

Fig. III.5 Buccaneer from Alexandre Olivier Exquemelin, *Histoire des avanturiers* (1686). Depiction of a buccaneer from Exquemelin's best seller. Buccaneers hunted wild pigs and cattle for meat and especially for their valuable hides. They often supplemented their purses by audacious raids on Spanish—or anyone else's—shipping.

contradicted the notion that only social scum emigrated. The same message pervaded the "Description de St. Christophe" (in Justel's *Recueil*) [61], and the booming popularity of buccaneer tales in the 1680s also made the Caribbean more alluring. By far the most famous of these sea-rovers' adventures was Alexandre Exquemelin's [Oexmelin] *Histoire des avanturiers* (Paris, 1686) [65]. Within the context of moral condemnation of the freebooters, he described an exciting life of adventure and heroic exploits against the Spaniards, spiced by tales of free love.

The burgeoning interest in the islands as military bastions dovetailed nicely with plans to profit from the Spanish succession crisis. The last Spanish Habsburg Charles II was sickly and childless, and the Bourbons had a claim to the throne through Louis's Spanish wife. Spanish alliance with the Dutch in the Dutch War (1672–78) fueled French plots to conquer New Spain. In 1676, Colbert sponsored the publication of Thomas Gage's famous exposé of Spain's purported vulnerability in the New World (*Nouvelle relation*, Paris, 1676) [66]. It was Colbert, also, who engaged the elderly novelist Gomberville [62] to translate the Spanish Jesuit Acuña's important early account of the Amazon as a potential route to Peru. The editor of the volume was frank about his purpose of providing a guidebook to the Peruvian heart of the Spanish Empire.

French government policies toward the English overseas were not as hostile as toward the Dutch and Spanish. After the short 1666–67 war, friendly relations with the later Stuarts (Charles II, 1660–1685; James II, 1685–1688) led to relative peace overseas. Irritations there were, as each side procrastinated about fulfilling the provisions of the Treaty of Breda concerning Acadia and St. Christopher. Though the English allied with the Dutch in 1674, not much Anglo-French fighting occurred overseas. After 1678, a long negotiation led to the important if short-lived Neutrality Treaty of 1687. This *Traité de Neutralité* (Bordeaux, 1687) [67] outlawed the use of Indian auxiliaries and of buccaneers.

In New France, there was innovation and expansion during the years between 1663, when the franchise of the Company of New France ended, and 1689, when war with England occurred. Although significant gains in population had been achieved from 1652 to 1663, in the years between 1665 and 1672 the population doubled from some 3,200 to about 7,000. Orphan girls sailed to the St. Lawrence at royal expense, and some four hundred soldiers of the Carignan-Salières regiment took advantage of bonuses and free land to settle there. The Jesuit *Relations* of the 1660s attest to the excitement of this population growth. Although there were probably more Frenchmen in Martinique, the demographic spurt of New France laid the foundation for the future Francophone population of the North American continent.

By 1664–65, Colbert reached conclusions about New France's role in the empire that would guide him and his son Seignelay. On the last leg of his imperial proconsulship, Tracy proceeded to the St. Lawrence in 1665 to deal with the Iroquois, and his successful campaign secured a tenuous peace that lasted until 1682. Also in 1665, Colbert sent Jean Talon to New France as intendant and chief agent for internal colonial development. With the Iroquois under control, the colonists would be able to set down roots all along the St. Lawrence. In Colbert's vision, most French colonists would become stable, prosperous small farmers and, with the stimulus of government subsidies, produce large families. Rents and tithes were kept substantially below those of France. Colbert admonished Talon to treat the people as a kindly, if strict, *père de famille*. He was to promote and even subsidize the production of timber, hardware, and provisions needed in the French islands. By 1672 when Talon was recalled and Colbert could no longer provide significant developmental funds, they had partially realized their goal of transforming a "crude, savage, and pagan" land into one that was "refined, happy, and Christian."

Colbert's plans for New France failed, however, to solve several significant problems that emerged in the 1660s and 1670s. These difficulties were all related to the fur trade, the principal export commodity of New France. Colbert wanted to restrict this commerce because it threatened to destroy the kind of compact colony that was his ideal for New France. The truce with the Iroquois, however, made it possible for French traders to travel to the region of the Great Lakes. The West and its potential riches held a great allure to young French Canadians little interested in the routinized life of farmer. Even Talon in his second tour as intendant (1670–72) pushed a western expansion policy by supporting Louis Joliet's exploration of Lake Ontario. The Jesuit Claude Dablon's *Relation de ce qui s'est passé le plus remarquable* of 1670–1671 (Paris, 1672) [68] attested to the attractions of the West and vented rumors about the Mississippi River.

The issue of the West came to a head during the Comte de Frontenac's first governorship (1672–82). Like Tracy, this veteran of European wars was a strong and dynamic personality. Like de Baas, he was not fearful of pursuing policies that went beyond or even contrary to his orders. Frontenac promoted the establishment of strongholds in the Great Lakes area, especially Fort Frontenac on Lake Ontario, to attract western furs away from the Iroquois middlemen. That he also profited personally from this

diversion did not diminish his enthusiasm for the West.

Frontenac sponsored systematic exploration of the West, including Louis Joliet and Jacques Marquette's historic voyage down the Mississippi to the Arkansas River. On their return, they took a shortcut up the Illinois River to the Chicago portage and through Lake Michigan home. Unfortunately, Joliet's maps and Marquette's manuscripts were lost near the end of the voyage, but Joliet later made a map from memory (one of the John Carter Brown Library's most esteemed treasures) [69] and Marquette's "Descouverte de quelques pays" appeared in Thévenot's *Recueil de voyages* (Paris, 1681) [70]. Also active in the Illinois country during the 1670s was Frontenac's protégé, René Robert Cavelier de La Salle.

These western initiatives caused hesitation in Paris and consternation in Bishop Laval's residence at Quebec. In 1676, Frontenac was ordered to halt western expansion. Colbert feared that the attractions of the woods-rovers' life would weaken the colony's farming base, and Laval was concerned that the brandy that lubricated the trade was causing great moral offenses. When Laval used excommunication against liquor peddlers in the West, Frontenac responded by assembling the so-called Brandy Parliament of 1678, which issued a compromise banning liquor in the West but allowing its distribution along the St. Lawrence. The bickering between Frontenac and a clique led by Laval and intendant Duchesneau continued until an annoyed king recalled the governor and intendant in 1682.

Laval's strength in this confrontation derived from the past achievements of the Church in New France and the bishop's authoritarian control of it. All parish priests received their training at Laval's Quebec seminary, and he had the strong support of

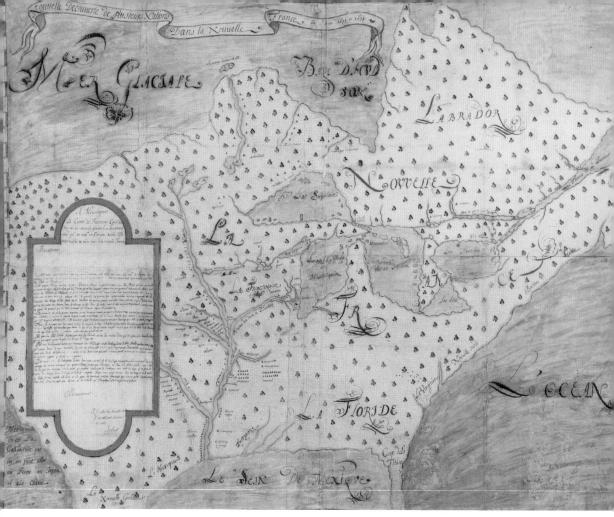

Fig. III.6 "Nouvelle découverte...dans la Nouvelle France" by Joliet (1674). Louis Joliet's drawing from memory of the course of the Illinois and Mississippi rivers. Reaching as far south as the confluence of the Arkansas and Mississippi rivers, Joliet and Father Marquette returned to the St. Lawrence only to lose drawings and notes when their canoe overturned. This manuscript map is one of the most precious possessions of the John Carter Brown Library.

Jesuits, Ursulines, and minor orders. He had even been able to levy a tithe, although it was worth less than fifty percent of the equivalent French burden. Not least important, Laval maintained powerful friendships at court, including that of Louis XIV. Even Colbert was utterly circumspect in trying to curtail the bishop's authority.

The emerging character of New France's society was one fraught with contradictions. While the young *Canadiens* took to the woods with their air of liberty, Laval attempted to forge a morally strict, tightly controlled community. He railed against those who countenanced balls with mixed-sex dancing. Benevolent royal officials struggled to regulate the minutiae of life in an environment strongly influenced by centrifugal forces. Later saddled with a reputation as a colony in the grips of governmental and ecclesiastical tyranny, New France's pioneers in fact obeyed only those laws harmonious with their vital interests, even while granting deference and respect to lay and clerical superiors.

It is misleading to characterize New France as a "feudal" society. "Feudalism" in Europe depended on warriors' control of agricultural laborers to provide a surplus; such conditions did not exist on the St. Lawrence. Many *seigneurs* (lords) did hold fine concessions, but they found it difficult to attract laborers. Those farmers who worked seigneurial lands paid very low dues, so meager, in fact, that historians emphasize the social rather than the economic value of these *seigneuries*. French Canadians even refused to be called peasants, preferring instead the proud term *habitant*.

The evangelical intensity of the earlier period declined in these decades. There were no more sensational Jesuit martyrdoms nor, after 1672, more of the invaluable Jesuit relations. The government's and the missionaries' concept of evangelization increasingly diverged. The official view emphasized the political value of missionaries who were to act as government agents holding the Indians to the French alliance. Christianity and the acculturation of the Indians to French civilization could not be divorced. Increasingly, the missionaries questioned this connection and argued for the isolation of their flocks on reservations far removed from the baneful influences of brandy and allied European vices. Even Governor Denonville had reached this conclusion by 1685, and the old vision of assimilation retained currency only at Versailles.

In the last years of his ministry, Colbert's ideal of a compact colony slipped even farther from reality, ironically in large measure

because of government policies. The establishment of a fur-monopoly company in France (1675), a financial expedient for the Crown, meant that Canadians could sell at a guaranteed price all the furs they could obtain. Traders streamed out to the West, with the number of *coureurs de bois* at least doubling between 1672 and 1682. Then, in 1678, La Salle persuaded Louis and Colbert to support his exploration of the Mississippi in return for the right to establish fur-trading posts in the Illinois country. In connivance with Frontenac, La Salle established forts on the St. Joseph, Illinois, and Mississippi rivers. La Salle's voyages provoked the Iroquois to launch attacks on the Illinois and Miami peoples in 1680. Who could doubt that the French would be the next target?

A new governor, Le Febvre de La Barre, former governor of Guiana, replaced Frontenac in 1682 with orders to respond to Iroquois attacks on France's Indian allies. The new leader's foray against the Iroquois was a barely disguised defeat. After La Barre's recall in disgrace (a not entirely deserved fate since the indolent Seignelay had not even read his frantic dispatches about French weakness in the West), Denonville, and then later Frontenac, would have to deal with the Iroquois menace for the rest of the century.

Much information about La Barre's and Denonville's Iroquois campaigns is provided in the popular *Nouveaux voyages* (The Hague, 1703, and later unauthorized editions) [71] by the celebrated Baron de Lahontan. His detractors have been legion because he included in his work so many obviously absurd claims, presumably to enhance sales and make himself look important. Nevertheless, Lahontan's eyewitness accounts of the Iroquois campaigns remain valuable. He admired the Canadians and claimed that it was their militia and not the regular troops that won victories against the

Fig. III.7 Map of "La Louisiane Gaspesie" from Chrétien Le Clercq, *Etablissement de la foy dans la Nouvelle France* (1691). This map, based on an earlier one (1688) by J. B. Franquelin, reflects La Salle's view—whether a result of error or of intent to deceive—of the distinctly southwestern course of the Mississippi. The mouth of the river is near Galveston, Texas.

tough Iroquois. Lahontan is also well known for his sympathetic accounts of Amerindian life; indeed, some commentators have seen in his work the source of the "noble savage" myth.

La Salle completed his two famous voyages during the 1680s. The first of 1682 took advantage of Joliet's and Marquette's route via the Illinois River. For the earliest part of this voyage the Recollect Father Louis Hennepin's *Description de la Louisiane* (Paris, 1683) [**72**] is of some value, although much of his work is unreliable because he did not accompany La Salle to the mouth of the Mississippi. After generally peaceful contacts with Amerindians along the river, the expedition reached the Gulf of Mexico. Under the name of another Recollect, Chrétien Le Clercq, a book was published in 1691 that claimed to be the journal of Father Zenobius Membré who accompanied the expedition. The account in "Le Clercq"'s *Etablissement de la foy* [**36**] is probably a composite of Membré's manuscript and other manuscript accounts.

On his return to Quebec, La Salle was confronted by the hostility of the new governor, La Barre. Leaving immediately for Paris, La Salle was somehow able to overcome the negative reports emanating from La Barre. To enhance his case, La Salle claimed that the Mississippi flowed into the Gulf near the Rio Grande, on the doorstep of Spain's silver empire. Since Louis and Seignelay were then giving high priority to an attack on Mexico as one response to Spain's declaration of war (1683), this information won their support for a second expedition. It should be added that contemporary geographers like J.B. Franquelin were taken in by the hoax. It is only fair to note that some scholars believe that genuine geographical error explains La Salle's actions.

La Salle's second voyage in 1684, by sea,

purposely landed beyond the Mississippi River at Matagorda Bay (Texas). The explorer searched inland for Spanish mines or, according to another viewpoint, for the Mississippi until an alienated clique conspired to murder this courageous, but strangely difficult, man. The survivors made it back to Canada to leave differing accounts of the expedition. Henri Joutel, one of La Salle's companions, published the *Journal historique du dernier voyage que feu M. de la Sale fit* (Paris, 1713) [73] to correct what he considered to be the falsifications, exaggerations, and inventions of Hennepin (1698) [74] and "Tonti" (1697). Disowned by its purported author, Henry de Tonti, the *Dernières découvertes dans l'Amérique septentrionale* (Paris, 1697) [75] recounts the desperate efforts to find La Salle's party. Also discussed in the pseudo-Tonti volume are the continuing French and Illinois struggles against the Iroquois in the late 1680s. Finally, Father Charlevoix's *Histoire et description générale de la Nouvelle France* (Paris, 1744) [76] gives a long description of La Salle's voyages based on critical use of previous accounts as well as unpublished manuscripts.

CHAPTER IV

War and Empire, 1689–1715

War against much of Europe characterized the last and increasingly difficult years of Louis XIV's reign. The contests in Europe are called the War of the League of Augsburg (1689–1697) and the War of the Spanish Succession (1701–1713). North Americans refer to them as King William's War and Queen Anne's War. England during this period emerged as France's most powerful rival, and the outbreak of war in Europe started a second Hundred Years' War. Between 1689 and 1815 France and Britain struggled for hegemony in a series of seven separate conflicts. The wars at the beginning (1689–1713) and the climax (1793–1815) of this long era were primarily struggles for dominance in Europe. Colonial and commercial supremacy was the catalyst for the mid-eighteenth-century (1739–1783) conflicts. But all of these struggles shaped the evolution of the French colonial empire.

During the War of the League of Augsburg, France and its colonies managed at least a stalemate against England. Despite the great defeat at La Hogue (1691), the French navy by 1695 reached the pinnacle of the buildup initiated by Colbert before starting a long if gradual decline. Also, effective French use of corsairs, and in the Caribbean of the buccaneers, supplemented naval operations during this war.

After Seignelay's death in 1690, Louis Phélypeaux de Pontchartrain assumed the ministry of the marine, and in 1693 his son Jérôme became co-minister. Because of war necessities, the Pontchartrains allowed governors and colonists to relax mercantilist rules governing *métropole*–colonial commercial relations. Foreign shippers found it easier to sell their cargoes in the Caribbean, and free trade in specific products like indigo was permitted.

After the Treaty of Ryswick (1697), Jérôme Pontchartrain, who became secretary of state for the *marine* but without ministerial rank, promoted a renewal of French power overseas. His imperial design focused on the disposition of Spain's American empire. With Charles II of Spain near death, Spain's colonies would devolve on France with a Bourbon succession, or if a hostile Austrian Habsburg candidate were chosen, France had to be ready to conquer Spanish America. In the short interwar period, 1697–1702, Louis XIV and Pontchartrain aggressively prepared France for the approaching contest. Island defenses were shored up, and the new Company for Saint Domingue (1698) had as one goal the strengthening of that western part of Hispaniola finally recognized at Ryswick as French. An expedition led by Pierre Le Moyne d'Iberville sailed to the Gulf Coast to establish a colony that would prevent a proposed English settlement there. Even more to the point, "Louisiana" would either protect a Spanish Empire that fell into Bourbon control, or in the event of a Habsburg succession, serve as a base for operations against New Spain (Mexico). Pontchartrain's final move occurred on the very eve of war when he permitted Antoine Laumet, called La Mothe Cadillac, to establish a fort at Detroit for protection of the route between New France and "Louisiana."

Historians have called Pontchartrain's program defensive imperialism or fortress imperialism. Although his chief advisor, the great fortifications expert Vauban, pushed him to develop the colonies, Pontchartrain lacked the power, financial support, and perhaps the will for such a task. He was not a member of the Royal Council, and he recognized that marginal gains in the Lowlands were more important to Louis XIV than all of his colonies. The War of the Spanish Succession meant decreases in the naval budget. Even beyond these unavoidable problems, Pontchartrain was less than optimistic about the future of colonization because he accepted the current view that France was underpopulated. Hence, during the war years when there were financial pressures, he concentrated on protecting shipping lanes to those areas of the Caribbean where French interests lay. His most important goal was the French commercial penetration of Spanish America. He considered colonies like New France burdensome and largely worthless.

French Guiana remained stagnant during this period. The luster of the early seventeenth century was a casualty of would-be millionaires dead of disease or of Amerindian arrows. From the recapture of Cayenne in 1677 to 1763, Guiana was a colonial backwater ignored by all save a few missionaries and naturalists. By the late seventeenth century, there were probably fewer than five hundred whites in the colony and not many more slaves. In his *Voyage de Marseille à Lima* (Paris, 1720) [77], Durret claimed that Cayenne did not have even four hundred inhabitants in 1711. There is a good description of Cayenne in the 1690s including a plan of the town in François Froger's *Relation d'un voyage de la Mer du Sud* (Amsterdam, 1715) [78]. The colony did only about one-twentieth the business of neighboring Dutch Guiana. French slavers rarely anchored at Cayenne, forcing the colonists to shop at the great Dutch slave emporium, Curaçao. Frenchmen at Cayenne grew a little sugar, indigo, and tobacco, and traded with the Amerindians. This tropical languor continued despite the energetic efforts of a string of outstanding governors from the Marquis de Férolles (1691–1705) through three successive members of the d'Orvilliers family.

The French Antilles fared better than any other colonies during these war years because the government viewed them as indispensable. Metropolitan strategic concerns especially favored the growth of Saint Domingue. The unleashing of a mixed force of regular troops and buccaneers against Cartagena in 1697 yielded an influx of specie at Saint Domingue. The sensational sack can be followed from the perspective of the French commander, J. B. Pointis (*Relation de l'expédition de Carthagène*, Amsterdam, 1698) [79]. Father Labat's *Nouveau voyage* (Paris, 1722) [63] related the story from the buccaneers' rather different point of view and gave credit for victory to their governor-commander, Jean-Baptiste Du Casse.

After Ryswick, a royal company undertook to develop the colony. Thanks to its intimate ties to Pontchartrain, this Company of Saint Domingue (1698) received permission to trade with Spanish Mexico. In 1701, the islands benefited from France's acquisition of the *asiento*, the privilege to trade slaves in the Spanish Empire. This contract only facilitated the already-prodigious amount of smuggling. It is not surprising to learn that colonists at Saint Domingue regulated their accounts in Spanish *reales* and *escuderos*.

The grave difficulty of providing adequate supplies from France during war years permitted island officials to ignore many trade regulations. The growth in the number of slaves during the war years is revealing. At Martinique and Guadeloupe, the number of slaves doubled. Increases were even more rapid at Saint Domingue, from about 9,000 slaves in 1700 to 24,000 in 1713; these figures do not include uncountable numbers of slaves resold to neighboring Spanish Santo Domingo. The islands did very well economically during these years.

The islands' startling growth however caused some troubling problems, especially the growing disproportion of blacks to whites. Pontchartrain attempted to diversify the island economies in ways that would reduce the need for black labor and to increase white population by requiring once more that merchants transport *engagés* (see Moreau de Saint-Méry) [39]. Royal officials simultaneously cracked down on mistreatment of indentured servants and legislated increasingly rigorous treatment of slaves, including restrictions on slaves' movements to prevent runaways (*marrons*) and on their carrying arms. Harsh treatment of slaves in these years was so pervasive that the king established ordinances (recorded in Moreau de Saint-Méry) [39] meant to enforce the Slave Code of 1685. Neither growing fear of racial imbalance nor even the occasional small slave revolts could alter planter greed.

Another problem of these years was the growing disparity in fortunes of the *grands* and *petits blancs* (planters and poor white farmers). The decline of tobacco in favor of more highly capitalized crops like indigo and sugar was the basic cause of this social rift. The small whites who engaged in buccaneering, coastal transport (*cabotage*), urban labor, and plantation administration were a volatile element whose hatreds included plantation owners, mulattoes, and blacks.

By 1713, Saint Domingue had propelled itself into a leading position among the French islands, a fact recognized a year later by the separation of its administration from that of the Lesser Antilles. But all of the islands emerged stronger during the war years, with the exception of St. Christopher, which became English at Utrecht. The loss of St. Christopher in the campaign of 1702 is recounted in Labat's *Nouveau voyage* [63].

Several contemporary accounts help to illuminate the character of island life in this era. A certain Monsieur N***'s *Voyages aux côtes de Guinée & en Amérique* (Amsterdam, 1719) [80] praised almost every aspect of Antillean life, except for the corrupt clergy. Life at Martinique yielded nothing to that of Europe, according to this author, and Guadeloupe would be a terrestrial paradise without its monks. It should be noted that the author greatly exaggerated island population. Gautier du Tronchoy's *Journal de la campagne des isles de l'Amérique* (Troyes, 1709) [81] contains a brief description of St. Christopher and Martinique in 1699. But by far the most useful and entertaining account is Labat's *Nouveau voyage* [63]. A former professor, this worldly Dominican arrived in the islands in 1693, and his colorful career there spanned the next twelve years. He established a prosperous sugar plantation, fought the English, and made a long visit to the rapidly declining Caribs at Dominica.

All this and much more, including important material on the islands' early history, he related in a lively, anecdotal style. The islands' major crops—sugar, tobacco, indigo, cotton—and the accompanying slave regime received detailed and intelligent treatment. Over three hundred pages are devoted to sugar alone. The slaves are described as temperamental, lascivious, and criminally oriented. Labat also provided various prescriptions for handling both new and seasoned Africans in order to avoid runaways and rebellion. While he advocated benevolent despotism, Labat especially cautioned owners to pay close attention to slave complaints. Labat gave detailed descriptions of island flora and fauna, accompanied profusely by illustrations. He depicted the Caribs with an amiable pen, denying that they were cannibals or cruel by nature. Yet, he flatly dismissed the possibility of converting them, a revealing admission from a man whose Dominican predecessors included Raymond Breton and Du Tertre.

The founding of Louisiana was an immediate consequence of Pontchartrain's defensive imperialism. Fears of English expansion in the southeast had been heightened by Louis Hennepin's *Nouveau voyage* (Utrecht, 1698) [74]. Dedicated to the English King William III, this often-spurious account of Hennepin's alleged voyages with La Salle provided the reader with an attractive picture of the vast interior of the North American continent. Daniel Coxe's reading of Hennepin (and of "Tonti"'s book) directly inspired his project to transport émigré Huguenots from England to the Mississippi. Iberville's expedition to the Gulf Coast was meant to forestall this English move as well as to establish a base near the heart of the Spanish Empire. Not surprisingly, many French translations of Spanish works about the New World appeared in the 1680s and 1690s. With regard to Louisiana, the most interesting is

Solís y Rivadeneyra's *Histoire de la conquête du Mexique* (Paris, 1684, 1691, 1705) [82]. Can it be a coincidence that this account of Mexico's riches first appeared in French in the year of La Salle's second voyage?

The first thirteen years (1699–1712) of Louisiana were saddled by such grave problems that its survival was almost a miracle. First and foremost, the War of the Spanish Succession left the Mobile settlement isolated, especially between 1708 and 1712 when war and famine wracked the *métropole*. Neither pay for the soldiers, goods for the colonists, nor new emigrants relieved the gloom of some two hundred soldiers and settlers. Only once did the king support the shipment of girls, twenty-two in 1704, quite unlike the case of New France in the 1660s. Pontchartrain, on principle, refused to consider convicts for the colony. Furthermore, the rule requiring ships to transport two *engagés* was suspended, not that many merchants paid call at Mobile. Finally, the governors of New France did everything in their power to prevent Canadian migration south.

False claims and unrealizable promises caused early enthusiasm for the colony to wane rapidly. The government officials, geographers, and adventurers who promoted the project believed La Salle's and Iberville's promises of gold mines and easy access to Spanish Mexico. As in the past, hardheaded merchants were not taken in by these illusions and played no role in the early years of the colony.

Potentially damaging to the colony in these first years was the difficulty of managing Amerindian relations. The small band of malaria-ridden colonists at Mobile, chosen as the site of the colony because the Tombigbee and Alabama rivers allowed access to the interior, were dangerously dependent on the powerful Choctaw nation for basic provisions and for security against England's Indian allies. Iberville, and after his death

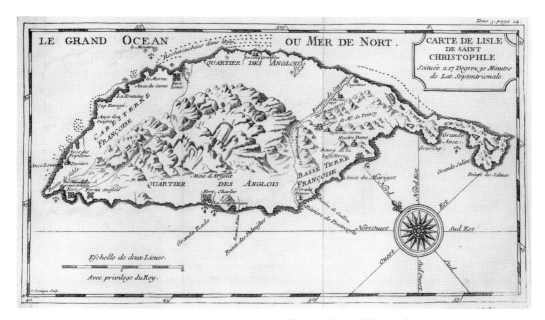

Fig. IV.I Map of L'Isle de Saint Christophe from Jean Baptiste Labat, *Nouveau voyage aux isles de l'Amérique* (1722). Published long after the English expelled the French from St. Christopher (or St. Kitts) in 1702, this map shows the division of the island. Except for a brief period of conflict, the neighbors had managed to coexist peacefully for more than a half century before 1688.

his younger brother Bienville, both good sons of New France, espoused the tried and true Indian policy of Canada. "Priests, posts, and presents" accompanied by amicable and just relations with allies, and harsh actions against enemies summarizes this policy. But Louisiana was short of priests and, worse, did not regularly receive from France the presents so necessary to smooth relations. Near-starvation forced Bienville to send his people into the woods to live among the Indians. The situation deteriorated further when English traders, especially Thomas Nairne, flooded the Southeast with quantities of cheap commodities. In 1708, Nairne even visited the Choctaws hoping to turn them against the beleaguered French; failing that, he intended to send the pro-English Chickasaws against the Choctaws. Fortunately for Mobile, Nairne quarreled with the governor of the Carolinas and was arrested. Even at this time, many southeastern Indians were growing disenchanted with the English failure to use the "present" system and with their increasing slave raids. In truth, English bungling allowed Bienville to

consolidate Louisiana's position vis-à-vis the Choctaw and the Alabamas. By 1720, perhaps one-third of the southeastern Indians gravitated toward the French camp, one-third deferred to the British, and one-third, the lower Creeks, were neutral. These attachments, which the Europeans fancied as alliances, were however very tenuous.

Another factor enabling Mobile to survive these years was its generally friendly relations with the Spanish colony at neighboring Pensacola, founded in 1698 to forestall French probes of the Gulf Coast. Both settlements were in desperate condition during the War of the Spanish Succession, and they succored each other when possible. But not all was sweetness between the Bourbon allies in North America. To the west, French expeditions that established trading posts on the Red River caused Spanish countermoves in Texas. This initial ambivalence between French and Spanish colonies characterized the era of French Louisiana (1699–1763).

By 1712, Ponchartrain found a solution to the Louisiana problem. He persuaded La Mothe Cadillac, the unscrupulous and corrupt former commandant at Detroit, to "sell" the colony to the super-rich financier Antoine Crozat. This Croesus-like money man had participated in previous commercial companies for the East Indies, South Seas, Guinea, and Saint Domingue trades. Relying on Cadillac's promises of mineral wealth, Crozat bought the colony. In return for a fifteen-year monopoly of its trade and a host of other privileges, he incurred few obligations. Cadillac, a partner with Crozat, became governor.

The Crozat proprietorship brought some immediate relief to Mobile but was of little aid to Louisiana's long-term health. The new owner had no intention of fulfilling even the minimal obligation to transport twenty colonists a year; instead, he intended to extract quickly whatever profit he could. Prices for his goods were high, and he tendered low offers for the colony's deerskins. He begrudgingly paid the colony's soldiers and officials but refused to consider honoring demands for back pay. When the promised mines went undiscovered and his hopes to establish trade with Spanish Veracruz were stymied, Crozat lost his enthusiasm and, as a good capitalist, cut his losses.

In Louisiana, the governorship of the arrogant and incompetent Cadillac proved nearly fatal. He quickly became enemies with the *commissaire-ordonnateur* (official in charge of royal finances and administration) Duclos and with the former governor Bienville. Cadillac's Indian policy departed

from Bienville's approach in that he offered low prices for Indian deerskins. Cadillac refused to give annual presents, and on occasion even balked at smoking the peace pipe. Fortunately, a long visit by Cadillac to the Illinois country allowed Bienville to redress Amerindian grievances. Thanks to their greater hostility to the English, the Choctaws maintained their French alliance and the Alabamas even allowed Bienville to establish the strategically placed Fort Toulouse at the juncture of the Coosa and Tallapoosa Rivers in modern, east central Alabama. Other garrisons were established in these years, for example on the Mississippi at Natchez (Fort Rosalie). These French gains were made possible by the Yamassee War (1715) against Carolina, which for several years severed British trade connections with the southeastern Indians. As a result, the previously precarious situation of Mobile was overcome, thanks to British ineptitude.

New France entered the war years in a vulnerable position. The previous two decades of westward expansion based on isolated garrisons linked together by *coureurs de bois* and protected by Amerindian allies left the colony exposed to Iroquois attacks. Following a debilitating smallpox epidemic in 1689, French settlements were ravaged by the Iroquois, notably La Chine on the threshold of Montreal. Even the return of the aged Frontenac in 1690 was not entirely a blessing because the western Indian allies and some Canadians accused him of pusillanimity toward the Iroquois to protect his fur-trade operations.

Fortunately, the colony had matured to the point of being capable of protecting itself. While regular troops fortified garrisons along the St. Lawrence, Canadian militia led by native-born officers fought an effective guerrilla war against the Iroquois until Frontenac could be persuaded to launch a frontal assault on the enemy villages in 1696. The Canadian officers also attempted to persuade the governor to destroy Albany, the supply post of the Iroquois, but he opted to send three war parties to New York and New England. Not only was Albany spared, but the strikes against peaceable New England farmers prompted an Anglo-American expedition against Quebec. This first assault on Quebec since 1628, described from the French perspective in *Relation de ce qui s'est passé en Canada* ([La Rochelle, 1691]) [83], failed ignominiously at the cost of 450 English lives. This debacle before Quebec was a major factor in the growing Canadian disdain of Anglo-American martial qualities.

Ironically, with the gratifying news of the 1696 campaigns against the Iroquois came strange tidings from Pontchartrain ordering the immediate abandonment of the western posts. A beaver fur glut in France was ruining the monopoly Company of the Farm, and the king could not afford to lose the cash the company paid to him. Hence the Canadians were expected to return to the situation prior to 1670 when Amerindians transported the furs to Montreal. At the same time, the company's guaranteed price for furs was radically reduced. This astonishing order alienated most elements of Canadian society except the clerics. Outcries from the colony led to a compromise by which four western posts would be maintained. This solution put the fur trade solely in the governor's hands and so naturally those left out became smugglers.

The situation deteriorated further in the years of peace, 1697–1702. After Frontenac died in 1698, one of his protégés, Cadillac, persuaded Pontchartrain to center French operations in the West at Detroit and to persuade Indian allies to settle there. Presumably a powerful fortress at Detroit would inhibit English expansion across the Appalachians. Not only did Cadillac proceed to exploit unmercifully both French and Indians, but Detroit's location placed France's Indian allies in close proximity to the Iroquois. When in 1701 the historic treaty of peace between France and the Iroquois nations was signed, there was little to prevent France's Amerindian allies from trading directly with Albany. In another of the many ironies of this period, the subjugation of the Iroquois threatened the French dominance of the Great Lakes trade. It now became clear that it was mainly the hostilities with the Iroquois that funneled much of the western fur trade to Montreal. Nor was it only the Indian allies who now found it possible to traverse Iroquois country; the *coureurs de bois* also found Albany receptive to their smuggled furs.

The War of the Spanish Succession affected different parts of New France differently. The New York-Iroquoian frontier was quiet because neither the new French governor, the Marquis Pierre de Rigaud de Vaudreuil (1703–1725), nor the English governor wanted war. Vaudreuil dreaded the revival of Iroquois hostilities, and he wanted to use the peace to strengthen western posts, especially Michilimackinac at the juncture of Lakes Michigan, Huron, and Superior. The situation, however, was very different in Acadia and New England, where Vaudreuil believed an aggressive policy was necessary to protect the weak French position. The neglected settlements in Acadia contained only a little more than 1,100 Frenchmen and thus were dependent on allied Abenakis, Micmacs, and Malecites. If these Indians made peace with the English, the colonists would be at the mercy of the New Englanders. It was imperative for Vaudreuil to goad his Indian allies to attack, and his success prompted French and Indian assaults from Deerfield in western Massachusetts to southern Maine. The frontier was ablaze. The inevitable revenge occurred in 1709 and 1710 when Anglo-American expeditions launched successful seaborne invasions of the Port Royal (Annapolis, Nova Scotia) region. Another attack on

New France in 1711 ended in disaster, however. Despite the lack of sustained aid from France, the Canadian colony survived the war years. True, at the Peace of Utrecht (1713), much was lost, but nothing essential. The area around Port Royal became English, but French influence on the Indians in Maine kept the land-hungry English south of the Kennebec River. Newfoundland was ceded to Britain but the "French shore" was retained to provide facilities for dry fishing. Britain gained sovereignty over Hudson Bay, but the Canadians soon found ways to discourage western Indians from trading furs there. Finally, article 15 of the Treaty gave the Anglo-Americans the right to trade freely in the West, but it was not worth the paper on which it was written.

Many authors who discussed New France in this era were former soldiers, and their experiences in Canada generated high praise for the vigorous people there. Lahontan's [71] favorable commentary was later echoed in Le Beau's *Avantures* (Amsterdam, 1738) [84], which asserted without irony that Canadians combined European morals with Amerindian physical skills. Le Beau noted the colony's growing reverence of military status, while savaging Lahontan's assertion that the Carignan-Salières soldiers had married women of low repute (*filles de joie*). In his *Histoire de l'Amérique septentrionale* (Paris, 1722) [85], Bacqueville de la Potherie provides details of the war years not found elsewhere. Interestingly, he not only understood Iroquois diplomatic and economic policies that were designed to retain control over the fur trade south of the Great Lakes, but he attempted to soften negative stereotypes of these perennial enemies.

The best early history of New France, *Histoire et description générale de la Nouvelle France* [76], by Father Charlevoix, is in a class by itself. This Jesuit spent four years at Quebec and later in 1720–1721 undertook a tour of the American colonies for the regent. He had access to archival documents through his relationship with the Comte de Maurepas, secretary of state (1725–38) and later minister of the marine (1738–49), and he read all previous works. While this thoroughness did little to eradicate his prejudices against the Huguenots and other opponents of the Jesuits, Charlevoix's detailed history has been an invaluable source for later historians. His book contains long sections on New France's flora and fauna and on aboriginal and European populations, as well as a detailed chronology. In general, he portrayed Canadian society favorably.

Fig. IV.2 "Canadien en raquette" from Claude-Charles Le Roy Bacqueville de La Potherie, *Histoire de l'Amérique septentrionale* (1722).
A Canadian off to war on snowshoes. The Canadian militia was a powerful striking force in the colonial wars after 1688.

CHAPTER V

Apogee and Catastrophe, 1715–1763

AFTER THE PEACE of Utrecht in 1713, the colonies were blessed by more than three decades of peace before the War of the Austrian Succession (1740–1748) and before the epic struggle for world commercial dominance with Britain during the Seven Years' War (1756–1763). With France and with much of Europe, the colonies enjoyed substantial demographic and economic growth. Between 1710 and 1750, the value of colonial trade jumped from 25 to 140 million *livres*. The Antilles, especially Saint Domingue, became the world's most valuable colonies. By 1750, some six hundred ships annually serviced the islands. Slave traders worked feverishly to provide the human material hellishly consumed in this era of sustained growth. New France lagged far behind in economic importance, but it outstripped the islands in growth of white population. The years after 1714 saw a rebound of fur prices, and greater progress was made in New France's commercial exchanges with the West Indies. In 1750 about twenty ships from France called at the St. Lawrence. Guiana and Louisiana remained poor orphans without adequate commercial contacts and slaves. Still, both colonies, especially Louisiana, made tangible progress.

In general, Versailles continued to follow the basic policies of Colbert as amended by Pontchartrain, except during the regency of the Duc of Orléans (1715–1723). Philippe, duc d'Orléans attempted to restore the nobility to real, administrative power, but he failed. His priorities so neglected the colonies that one historian has recently labeled them his "no colonies policy," although occasional regency initiatives like the beginning of the North Atlantic fortress Louisbourg should not be forgotten. The navy, already in decline, deteriorated still further as its funds decreased from 15 million *livres* in 1715 to 4.5 million in 1718. The Regent, apparently viewing the colonies as receptacles for France's undesirables, reestablished the *forçat* policy. In 1718, he ordered the arrest and deportation to the colonies of vagabonds in the Paris region. Two years later, beggars all over France were given the same sentence. These draconian laws were overturned in 1720 only after outraged protests in France and in the colonies. (Copies of these edicts are available at the John Carter Brown Library.) The regency's policies caused considerable damage to the reputation of the colonies.

The regent's indifference to the colonies allowed his favorite, the Scottish financier John Law, to consolidate all previous commercial companies into the gigantic Company of the Indies (1720). This company swallowed the East Indies company, African slave-trade companies, and Law's own Company of the West (1717) for the colonization of Louisiana. The new company was to provide the backing for Law's fantastic banking operations intended to liquidate the national debt. Despite the crash of Law's bank in 1720, the Company of the West remained in operation until 1731.

With the maturity of Louis XV in 1723, the earlier administrative apparatus regained favor. Jean-Frédéric Phélypeaux, the Comte de Maurepas, headed the *Marine* from 1725–1749, and the Bureau of the Colonies established by Pontchartrain in 1710 grew in importance. Maurepas, the son of Jérôme Pontchartrain, generally followed the outlines established by Colbert and his father. The islands were the jewels of the empire, and the mainland colonies provided the setting. Instructing a Canadian intendant, the minister urged him to wean the colonists from excessive hunting and trapping, to stimulate the production of flour, peas, timber, and fish for trade with the islands, and to promote shipbuilding and mining. One might as well be reading the correspondence of Colbert and Talon. Always short of cash, Maurepas counseled caution about colonial expansion, although he did support the Pontchartrain policy of building or strengthening vital fortresses. The completion of Louisbourg at Cape Breton, built to guard the Gulf of St. Lawrence, is a prime example.

The most neglected colony in this period was Guiana, where only about six hundred French lived in 1760, most of them in the squalid town of Cayenne. At most, one or two ships could be expected to visit annually to pick up meager quantities of sugar, indigo, and tobacco. About three thousand slaves toiled in the fields. What paltry results for the previous century's efforts there!

Guiana suffered from the circular problem of colonial poverty. Slavers bypassed it for richer colonies, and the shortage of slaves stifled progress in draining wetlands. The various Amerindian groups traded hammocks and provisions with the colony, but they produced no indispensable export commodity like the furs of New France. European diseases ravaged the Indians and local afflictions, particularly yellow fever, consumed the Europeans. Further hampering the colony was its miserable reputation, the product of repeated disasters. Ministers saw no profit in promoting it, and in a century of French-Spanish alliance its strategic importance was negligible.

To relieve this dismal picture, there were a few, faint signs of hope. From 1704 to 1762 Rémy d'Orvilliers and two later d'Orvilliers did everything in their power to protect the aborigines from unscrupulous French traders, and always followed the policy of treating them as independent nations. These policies, which dated back to Colbert and Le Febvre de La Barre, are remarkable in that the French had less to gain from such benign conduct than in New France. The scattered aboriginal remnants posed little threat and their trade, while useful, was not crucial. Louis XV (1723–1774) backed up this policy by unequivocal condemnations of Amerindian slavery.

The Jesuit missions of this era provided little islands of economic prosperity and, more debatably, of enlightenment. About ten Jesuits serviced the houses at Kourou and St. Paul on the Oyapok River. Father Lombard established the Kourou residence in 1710 and by 1736 some six hundred Indians had domiciled there. These paternalistic communities sought with little success to evangelize the aborigines and with greater success to protect them from Europeans. With their eight hundred slaves, these *reducciones* prospered economically until the Jesuits were expelled from Guiana.

Despite the miseries of Guiana, it attracted a significant number of voyagers, scientists, and propagandists. In the latter category, Father Labat published his *Voyage du chevalier des Marchais en Guinée...et à Cayenne* (Amsterdam, 1731) [86] to stimulate colonization. Typically, he denied that climate, soil conditions, or disease prevented European settlements there and pointed to Dutch successes at Guiana. He excoriated those who advocated a *forçat* policy and instead called for voluntary emigration of *petits blancs* from overcrowded Martinique. Labat presented a long history of the colony to demonstrate that poor planning and incompetent leadership had frustrated colonization. Sympathetic to the aborigines, he applauded the hands-off policy toward them. Although Labat did not visit Guiana, he employed the available printed sources and made use of important manuscript sources such as a letter from Father Lombard at Kourou. The remarkable books of the Dominican Labat in conjunction with those of the Jesuit Charlevoix gave French readers of the period a history of the French colonies in America unsurpassed until the twentieth century.

The era of the French scientific voyager started in the 1690s with Father Plumier's famous study of Antillean botany (*Description des plantes de l'Amérique*, Paris, 1693) [87]. Tropical Guiana's exuberant flora and fauna were particularly attractive to the curious intellect. La Condamine published his *Relation abrégée d'un voyage* (Paris, 1745) [88] and Pierre Barrère his *Nouvelle relation de la France équinoxiale* (Paris, 1743) [89]. The royal botanist at Cayenne, Barrère exposed realistically the economic and medical problems of Guiana. However, these difficulties could be overcome if Cayenne had a larger popu-

lation, and Barrère sought to attract prospective colonists by demonstrating in detail how to construct a sugar plantation. If enough new settlers became successful planters, then merchant ships would regularly visit Cayenne, breaking the cycle of misery. Beyond elaborating this now-traditional analysis, Barrère presented the reader with many curious observations and pictures of Guiana's plants, animals, and aborigines.

The islands had experienced economic growth during the war years (1689–1713), but after Utrecht they boomed. Peace meant easier access to French markets. Peace, however, also meant the return of the *Exclusif*, the *métropole*'s "mercantilist" control of the colonial economy. Even so, the colonists used rebellions, bribery of officials, and smuggling to gain access to foreign markets. The fact that the King repeatedly ordered enforcement of laws prohibiting foreign trade suggests the scope of the problem.

Various statistics demonstrate the islands' economic growth. Both white and black populations increased significantly. The number of whites at Martinique jumped from 4,770 in 1683 to 14,000 in 1756, which certainly shows that not all maturing sugar colonies had declining European populations. Between 1713 and 1753 the number of slaves at Martinique and Guadeloupe soared from 14,500 to 65,000, and at Saint Domingue from 24,100 in 1717 to 172,000 in 1752. The number of sugar plantations at Saint Domingue increased from 340 to 600 between 1730 and 1750, and in all the islands cotton and especially coffee became major export crops. By 1755, the French islands produced almost as much sugar as the British, and because of its cheaper price French sugar dominated European markets.

French commerce with the islands after 1713 grew dramatically until war with Britain started to take its toll after 1744. But even an extraordinary increase of French shipping did not stop the islanders' dependence on foreign shipping. Crucial in these years was the growth of illicit trade with the "Bostonians," the islanders' name for Anglo-Americans. Despite some increase of Canadian ships trading in the Antilles, the islanders depended on the Anglo-Americans for salt-fish, timber, flour, and peas. Despite edicts like that of 1727 (see Moreau de Saint-Méry) [39] nothing could halt a trade so beneficial to both partners. The "Bostonians" had excellent reasons for trading with the French islands: cheap sugar and great quantities of molasses and *tafia* fueled their booming rum distilleries. British regulations forced the English islanders to send the molasses-laden brown sugar home. French regulations forbade the export of rum to France because of the potential injury to the wine and brandy trades.

By a variety of means, the islanders softened the impact of the *Exclusif*. Most dramatic were the rebellions between the years 1717 and 1723. At Martinique, the colonials greeted the Regent's attempt to raise taxes by forcibly embarking the governor and intendant on a voyage to France. The Superior Council at Martinique immediately opened island trade to foreigners. This so-called Gaoulé revolt achieved success when the duc d'Orléans responded by disgracing the poor royal officials. When the Company of the West attempted in 1721 to enforce the *Exclusif* at Saint Domingue, the planters evicted the royal officials, instituted free trade, and abolished taxes. Only two rebels paid with their lives after a royal fleet restored control in 1722, and Louis XV's accession to the throne in 1723 occasioned a general amnesty. Father Charlevoix, at Saint Domingue in 1721 at the end of his colonial tour, witnessed the beginning of the revolt and provided a long account in his *Histoire de l'isle espagnole ou de S. Domingue* (Paris, 1730–

Fig. v.1 "Isles de l'Amérique"
from Pierre-François-Xavier
de Charlevoix, *Histoire de l'isle
espagnole ou de S. Domingue*
(1730–1731).
A map depicting French possessions in Lower Louisiana
and in the islands, as well as
the Spanish colonies in the
Caribbean that were so attractive to eighteenth-century
traders and smugglers.

Fig. v.2 Map of "La Louisiane" from Le Page du Pratz, *Histoire de Louisiane* (1758).

As this map illustrates, "Louisiana" included the heartland of North America from roughly the Appalachians to the Rockies. French explorers and traders had by this time (1757) penetrated far west of the Mississippi along the Red River and Missouri River basins. The obvious propaganda intent of this document is demonstrated by numerous references to mines.

1731) [90]. Recent historians, however, do not accept his view that the *petits blancs* were responsible for the rebellion, instead seeing them as agents of the *grands blancs*. Another account, "Memoire sur la revolte," written in 1750 but published in M. Bourgeois's *Voyages intéressans dans différentes colonies* (London, 1788) [91], blamed the Company of the West's unreasonable abuse of its monopoly powers.

Although rebellions were the most dramatic response to the *Exclusif*, smuggling was the normal act of resistance. Royal officials lacked the naval resources to suppress the *caboteurs*, the small boat operators who transferred goods at night from foreign ships. Furthermore, these officials had much to gain from laxity in enforcing edicts — unless Versailles heard about it. Their social milieu was the planter elite, and hence "unreasonable" enforcement of the *Exclusif* meant social ostracism. On occasion, the officials even tolerated colonial assemblies *à l'Anglaise*, much to the king's fury. After 1744 and the resumption of war, colonial officials often used the device of declaring an "emergency" in order to open ports to foreign shipping.

An increasing volume of slaves fueled the islands' economic boom. The French private slavers, no longer excluded by the monopoly companies of the Colbert-Pontchartrain era, supplied a large percentage of the 955,000 slaves imported during the eighteenth century. Large numbers also came from British slavers through Jamaica just across the Windward Passage from Saint Domingue. Dutch Curaçao helped supply the Lesser Antilles. This astonishing increase of Africans shaped eighteenth-century island society. Blacks rapidly increased their demographic dominance, outnumbering whites four to one at Martinique and six or seven to one at Saint Domingue by 1755. The whites promulgated "apartheid" laws to control the new arrivals. The relatively lenient provisions of the 1685 Black Code, meant to protect slave property at a time of shortages, rapidly gave way to more repressive measures. Increasing barriers to manumission were erected, and it even became difficult for masters to liberate their mulatto bastards. Freedmen, whether mulattoes or blacks, were increasingly subject to official and social prohibitions. Riot laws and prohibitions against integrated militia companies and cemeteries typified these tools of control.

Responses of slaves to growing repression varied but rarely included open revolt. At Saint Domingue, *marronage* (escape to a fugitive slave community) was a realistic response in that the rugged terrain and nearby sparsely inhabited Spanish Santo

Domingo provided relatively safe havens. *Marrons* were usually African, often newly arrived, subject to particularly harsh planters or to callous managers of absentee owners. Often, slaves fled when customary privileges, especially the right to maintain gardens, were withdrawn as punishment. Other responses included work slowdowns, tool breaking, arson, poisoning of other slaves, and suicides. All in all, the situation among the races was worse at booming, slave-devouring Saint Domingue than at the older, more established Lesser Antilles.

Various contemporary sources discuss the character of island life in this period. Monsieur N***'s *Voyages* [80] describes the hospitality of the planter elite early in the century. Ample if inexpensive foods and liquors were placed at the author's disposal during his tour. This colonial hospitality would become legendary as the planters' wealth increased throughout the century. However, Father Charlevoix [90] was much less enthusiastic about the planter lifestyle, especially their cavalier attitude toward religious duties. As noted above, he described the *petits blancs* as riotous and insolent. At the end of this period, Saintard in his *Essai sur les colonies françoises* on Saint Domingue (Paris, 1754) [92] complains of the islanders' "distaste for the *patrie* and love of foreign laws," referring to the Anglophilia of the planter elite. This characterization undoubtedly exaggerated the hostility toward France, but it is clear that the islanders intended to control the terms of the metropolitan connection.

Two distinct periods divide the history of Louisiana from the time of Crozat's ownership to the colony's cession to Spain in 1762. In the first, from 1717 to 1731, the Company of the West administered the colony; in the second, 1731 to 1762, Louisiana was a royal colony. The *Lettres patentes* (Paris, 1717) [93] issued to John Law's Company of the West granted it extraordinary powers on paper. It did not even have to pay the king a share of minerals discovered. Emigrants to Louisiana were exempt from all taxes for ten years! In return for these and many other privileges, the company accepted the obligation to transport six thousand whites and three thousand blacks over the twenty-five-year period of its monopoly. It also paid Crozat two million *livres* for his interests in the colony.

Recognizing the connection between long-term profitability and population growth, Law simultaneously accepted *forçats* and mounted a promotional crusade for free emigration. He persuaded the regent to issue orders transporting all idlers to Louisiana. For a time the Paris police were paid according to numbers arrested. This policy created so much opposition and so many rumors about the fate of missing persons that the Regent in an *Arrest du Conseil d'Estat du roy . . . à la Louisianne* (Paris, 1720) [**94**] admitted that the *forçat* policy was a big mistake.

The Company of the West orchestrated a slick propaganda campaign for Louisiana. In gazettes like the *Mercure de France*, Law's hired pens evoked visions of a promised land on the Mississippi. Not bothering with the more knowledgeable port towns of France, newspapers and posters promoting emigration flooded the interior French borderlands, especially Alsace and Lorraine, and the Rhineland and Switzerland. Propaganda accounts in German were a novel feature of Law's campaign. Some four thousand people believed the promises and headed for designated ports in France. At these reception centers, lack of facilities and food, as well as diseases fostered by the fetid conditions, contributed to some two thousand deaths.

Of the perhaps four thousand *forçats* and volunteers who reached the colony between 1718 and 1721, relatively few became permanent colonists. Some 2,500 were immobilized at the disembarkment camp at Biloxi for periods of up to a year, with the resulting mortality of hundreds of them. The Company had neither the resources nor the direction to manage such large migrations, and the poor colony could not start to supply the newcomers. The small minority of those who survived these traumas and settled along the Mississippi would later play an important role in the agricultural development of the colony. However, as the others returned home bitter and disillusioned, their stories badly sullied the colony's image. To most Frenchmen, Louisiana now emerged as a home of prostitutes and criminals. Whether deserved or not, this reputation made the future recruitment of colonists extremely difficult.

The colony was anything but prepared for new arrivals, since it barely supported its five hundred settlers. Pay for soldiers in these years was so low and infrequent that desertions, riots, and mutinies were common. A mutiny of soldiers at Fort Toulouse was suppressed only with the help of the Alabamas. Louisiana was without the resources to proffer significant aid to immigrants that the Company left largely in the lurch.

After Law's exile in 1720, the Company managed to struggle on until 1731. It moved the capital from Mobile to New Orleans in 1723. Although it never earned enough to fulfill its commitments, the Company did conduct a fairly lively deerskin trade in the 1720s. But the *coup de grâce* came with the destruction by the Natchez Indians of Fort Rosalie on the Mississippi. The last proprietary governor, Perrier, followed the anti-Indian policies of Cadillac; in particular, he refused to remove the French commandant at Fort Rosalie despite repeated complaints from the Natchez. In 1730, the angry Natchez retaliated by killing all French males and enslaving women, children, and blacks. This traumatic event led to the restoration of royal rule and the return to Bienville's Indian policy. A campaign of revenge destroyed Natchez autonomy.

Father Charlevoix's "Journal d'un voyage" in the third volume of his *Histoire... de la Nouvelle France* [76] contains interesting details about the Natchez settlement in 1721. Published in the *Recueil de voyages au Nord* (Amsterdam, 1725–1738) [95], the Jesuit Le Petit's "Relation des Natchez" is a detailed account of the Natchez tragedy. One of the most important relations of the era, Le Page du Pratz's *Histoire de Louisiane* (Paris, 1758) [96], presents a different perspective on the "massacre." A veteran of Louisiana and a resident at Natchez for eight years, the author blames the French commandant of Rosalie for the troubles because he refused to punish a young soldier for the murder of an elderly Natchez. This work contains much else, including descriptions of commodities and a long chapter on how to deal effectively with black slaves. Le Page du Pratz's friend Dumont de Montigny based his *Mémoires historiques sur la Louisiane* (Paris, 1753) [97] on his twenty-five years of military experience and his extensive travels. He wrote long, sympathetic passages on Amerindians that in some places sound like Jean-Jacques Rousseau. These *sauvages*, Montigny asserted, without arts, sciences, or luxuries, were happier than Europeans. In volume two the author discussed in great detail the Natchez "massacre." Another veteran of many years in Louisiana, the "lover of humanity" Captain Bossu, published a history of Louisiana from the 1720s in his *Nouveaux voyages aux Indes Occidentales* (Paris, 1768) [98]. His account of the Natchez events, for which he largely blames the French, was based in part on conversations with Natchez captives sold as slaves to Saint Domingue.

By 1730, significant French establishments were emerging in the Illinois country, in a hundred-kilometer area along the middle Mississippi. Building on early Jesuit mission sites at Cahokia (1699) and Kaskaskia (1703), prospectors and traders increased the French presence. But it was the Company of the West that promoted the development of an area it believed to be rich in minerals. The Company persuaded the government to include Illinois in its administration, much to Canada's and Vaudreuil's chagrin. Between 1719 and 1725 company soldiers, colonists, and miners dramatically increased the French presence. The first Fort de Chartres was constructed to protect the newly important settlements. However, failure to discover mines and conflicts with the Fox nation kept the population at about 325.

When Bienville returned to Louisiana as royal governor in 1733 after an absence of nine years, he was struck by the demographic and economic stagnancy of the colony. He returned just in time because British traders were making serious inroads among the Choctaws, that strong nation of some fifteen thousand on whom French security and economic vitality utterly depended. With the new colony of Georgia and its vigorous governor making overtures to the Choctaws, Louisiana was in mortal danger. Among the Choctaws, a faction led by Red Shoes argued for an English alliance. Bienville took vigorous countermeasures, especially the construction of Fort Tombecbe (1735) on the Tombigbee river. The Choctaws had long desired a trading post in their territory. He also rendered impartial justice to any Choctaw wronged by the French. But Bienville continued to be hampered by the shortages of trade goods and "presents," and his failed campaigns against the Chickasaws in 1736 and 1740 kept the French position precarious.

After the weary Bienville's retirement, his successor Pierre de Rigaud de Vaudreuil, son of the former Canadian governor, brought the struggle with the Choctaws to a head in

1746. In that year, with France and Britain at war, Red Shoes killed three French traders. Vaudreuil's intense pressure on the Choctaws for justice led to the death of Red Shoes and subsequently to a bitter civil war among the Choctaw that cost eight hundred lives. In the end, France retained the crucial Choctaw alliance.

The last years of the French regime saw some positive steps in the colony's development. Between 1748 and the start of the Seven Years' War, significant numbers of Alsatians, lured by attractive terms, settled in Louisiana. Then during the Seven Years' War, Louisiana benefited from shipping that could not land at blockaded ports in the Caribbean and at the St. Lawrence. At the same time, Governor Kerlerec secured the allegiance of almost all the southeastern Indians. Even the traditionally pro-British Cherokees were persuaded to attack the Carolinas in 1760, but they were soon to regret this allegiance to Louisiana.

Upper Louisiana as the Illinois country came to be known, grew steadily from the 1730s to 1762. Agriculturalists joined traders, missionaries, and soldiers, and significant numbers of slaves arrived through New Orleans. The growth of this port city provided an outlet for Upper Louisiana wheat and furs. Along with the older settlements, Sainte-Genevieve on the west bank thrived in these years.

Despite these signs of progress, Louis XV and the Duc de Choiseul relinquished Louisiana to Spain in 1762 as payment for entry in the Seven Years' War against Britain. That the French crown was spending eight hundred thousand *livres* a year maintaining the colony without tangible returns no doubt contributed to this decision. The dream of French control of the North American heartland had too often turned to nightmare. In France, few complained of the decision.

Marked economic and demographic growth characterized New France during the second quarter of the eighteenth century. Population increased from about twenty thousand to more than fifty-five thousand, despite very small numbers of French immigrants. Peace and prosperity explain this growth, which was chiefly due to natural increase. Peace, a rise in fur prices, and increasing economic diversification were principal factors in the colony's economic spurt. Under Maurepas and intelligent intendants like Gilles Hocquart, subsidies were accorded to shipbuilding and mining enterprises. Trade with the islands grew substantially. Measures were implemented to increase and retain wealth in New France. To stimulate the growth of a Canadian bourgeoisie, Hocquart favored colonial merchants over their metropolitan counterparts. In 1744, the king prohibited the establishment of new religious communities because these "withdraw from commerce a considerable part of the wealth of our colonies."

An opinionated but often-perceptive account of New France is the "Journal" of Charlevoix [76]. The Jesuit traveled from the mouth of the St. Lawrence to New Orleans reporting on subjects ranging from colonial mores to the habits of the beaver. Five letters of the Journal are devoted to the *sauvages*. Charlevoix's fellow Jesuit, Father Lafitau, published his very influential *Moeurs des sauvages amériquains* (Paris, 1724) [99], which also treats New France extensively. Within the rather unoriginal framework of comparing Amerindian culture with that of the ancient Greeks and Romans, Lafitau presented a massive compilation of information on primarily North American aborigines. Not the least interesting part of his work are the drawings. Somewhat later in 1750 the Swedish naturalist Pehr Kalm toured the St. Lawrence area. His *Travels into North America* (London, 1770–1771) [100], which did not receive a French translation presumably due to the loss of New France in 1763, provides an indispensable and favorable account of Canadian mores and material culture.

Security concerns remained paramount for New France, and its society had a distinctly military flavor. Faced with English gains at Utrecht, New France responded by expansion. North and west of Lake Superior, the construction of a system of trading posts inhibited the Amerindians from taking their furs to the Hudson Bay. The famous La Vérendrye, granted a post at Lake Nipigon north of Superior, reached the Rockies by 1745. Posts were established at Lake Winnipeg and beyond to Saskatchewan. South of the Great Lakes, the French were greatly concerned about English competition luring fur traders to Albany or, after 1724, to the even closer Fort Oswego at Lake Ontario.

Fig. v.3 "Port et ville de Louisbourg" from Pierre-François-Xavier de Charlevoix, *Histoire et description générale de la Nouvelle France* (1744). Plan of the naval bastion at Louisbourg on Cape Breton. Constructed following the Treaty of Utrecht (1713) to protect French merchants and the fishing fleet, Louisbourg proved vulnerable to English naval assaults (1745, 1758).

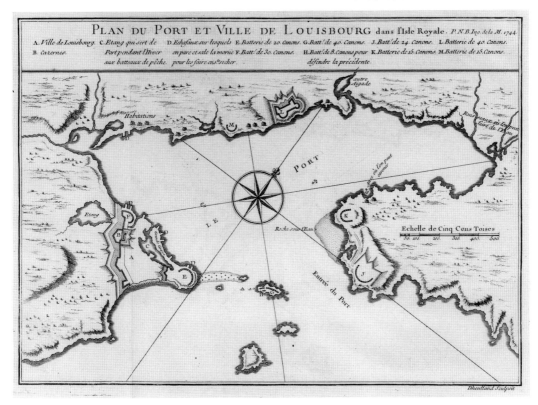

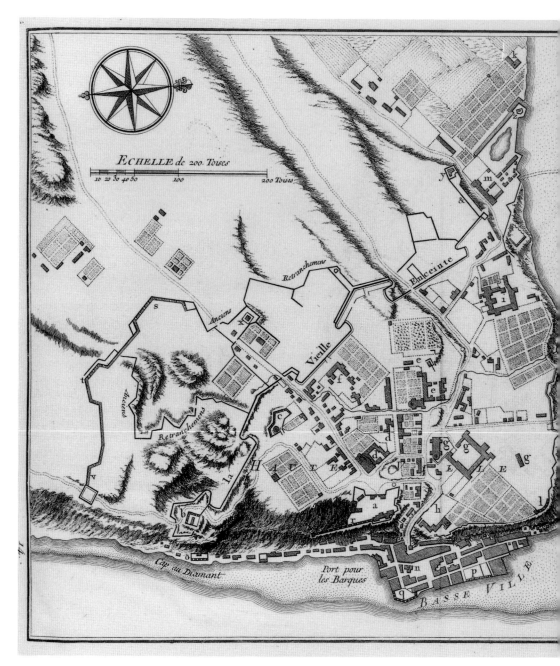

Fig. v.4 "Québec" from Pierre-François-Xavier de Charlevoix, *Histoire et description générale de la Nouvelle France* (1744). Plan of the town of Quebec, the political and military center of New France. Sitting on a heavily fortified rock overlooking the St. Lawrence, Quebec resisted assaults, except in 1629 and the final one of 1759.

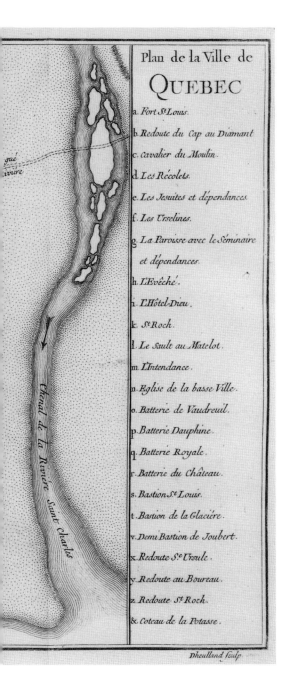

Plan de la Ville de

QUEBEC

a. *Fort St Louis.*

b. *Redoute du Cap au Diamant*

c. *Cavalier du Moulin.*

d. *Les Récolets.*

e. *Les Jesuites et dépendances.*

f. *Les Urselines.*

g. *La Paroisse avec le Séminaire et dépendances.*

h. *L'Evêché.*

i. *L'Hôtel-Dieu.*

k. *St Roch.*

l. *Le Sault au Matelot.*

m. *L'Intendance.*

n. *Eglise de la basse Ville.*

o. *Batterie de Vaudreuil.*

p. *Batterie Dauphine.*

q. *Batterie Royale.*

r. *Batterie du Château.*

s. *Bastion St Louis.*

t. *Bastion de la Glacière.*

v. *Demi Bastion de Joubert.*

x. *Redoute St Ursule.*

y. *Redoute au Boureau.*

z. *Redoute St Roch.*

&. *Coteau de la Potasse.*

Dheulland sculp.

The building up of Detroit was one response to the threat, but the need to subsidize trade goods there and at other posts to keep them competitive with the English cost the royal treasury dearly.

New France had one basic advantage in the struggle for the western fur trade. Canadian militia were able to attack nations hostile to the French and their Indian allies. In this period the main target was the Fox nation that lived in the area west of Lake Michigan. Successful assaults against these people not only much reduced their threat to French posts and trade routes but kept the Indian allies in line by demonstrating the long arm of the Quebec authorities.

The War of the Austrian Succession (1740–1748) caused multiple difficulties for New France, especially after the imposition of a partially effective British blockade in 1744. The shortages of trade goods became so serious by 1747 that the French position in the Great Lakes came close to collapse. Goaded by Iroquois emissaries, Indians discussed a general rising against New France. Only with the appearance of reenforcements and with the free flow of goods after the cessation of hostilities in 1748 did the situation stabilize. At the east end of New France, the naval bastion at Louisbourg, designed to protect the St. Lawrence, fell to a New England expedition supported by the royal navy. In response, the Canadians sent war parties into New York and New England to strike terror. At the peace treaty of Aix-La-Chapelle in 1748, France was for the first time willing to trade conquests in the Lowlands for gains in the New World, namely the reversion of Louisbourg.

The War of the Austrian Succession pointed up too well the weakness of the French colonial empire. Although Maurepas somewhat strengthened the navy during his long ministry, there could be little hope of matching the British given France's European priorities and given the navy's poor use of its assets. With contacts between the colonies and Paris always tenuous, New France's Indian alliances and thus its fur trade were vulnerable. Equally exposed were Guiana and Louisiana, whose only protection against British forces was the small value of their commerce. The Antilles were in a more favored position because Versailles gave them high priority, but any prolonged blockade had serious consequences for the islands.

After 1748, the most urgent area of French concern was the Anglo-American penetration of the Ohio River Valley and the increasing commercial contacts that the English established south of the Great Lakes. The new governor at Quebec, the talented Marquis de la Galissonière, recommended urgent measures to beef up the French presence in the Illinois country. Only that would keep the Indians loyal and prevent the dreaded English from severing the connection between New France and Louisiana. At the very time Galissonière was sending his dispatches to Versailles, Virginia planters and their London backers were forming the Ohio Company for the settlement of the valley. Indeed, the start of the Seven Years' War (1756–1763) occurred in North America in the upper Ohio Valley prior to official declarations. After failing to coerce the various Ohio River Indian nations into expelling Anglo-American traders, the French in 1752 decided to remove them forcibly. The new governor at Quebec, the Marquis de Duquesne, sent a force to construct forts from Lake Erie south to the Ohio headwaters. After two years of herculean labor, Fort Duquesne was constructed at present-day Pittsburgh. When the French garrison there humiliated the Virginia militia led by Colonel George Washington, the French

hold west of the Appalachians appeared impregnable.

Both sides now prepared for war. The British without the benefit of a declaration of war struck hard at French shipping. Then a regular force under General Braddock arrived in North America to provide backbone to the ragtag colonial militias. An assault on Fort Duquesne was to precede a sweep of French positions at Lakes Ontario and Champlain. In the same year, 1755, the English forcibly removed from Nova Scotia French settlers who were assumed to be disloyal to their new overlords. The cruel manner of their removal received extensive publicity in New France and inevitably fostered bitter resistance in the subsequent conflict. The John Carter Brown Library has many pamphlets about the Acadian controversy of these years.

The initial victories in this war went to the French. Some 250 Canadians with 600 Indian allies shattered Braddock's force near Fort Duquesne, and the routed English and Anglo-Americans straggled back to Virginia. French versions of this famous battle have been collected in the *Relations diverses sur la bataille de Malangueulé* (New York, 1860) [101] and in the *Relation de ce qui s'est passé cette année en Canada* (Paris, [1755]) [102]. The latter account also includes information on the successful defense of the Lake Champlain front against an English invasion force.

The newly appointed governor Pierre de Rigaud de Vaudreuil (called Vaudreuil-Cavagnal to distinguish this former governor of Louisiana from his celebrated father and former governor of New France) sent war parties against English frontier settlements from the Appalachians to the Atlantic. Even Fort Oswego was captured. In 1757, Fort William Henry at the foot of Lake George fell to the new commander of French forces, the Marquis de Montcalm. Albany immediately to the south and perhaps even New York City were laid open to French assaults. Nevertheless, 1757 marked the high tide of French successes.

Divisions within New France, especially between the arrogant Montcalm and the native-born Vaudreuil, bedeviled further operations. Whereas the governor wished to press the French advantage, the pessimistic Montcalm insisted on a defensive strategy. The hatreds between the French and Canadian officers reflected those of the Marquis and the governor. Eventually, Versailles sided with Montcalm. Meanwhile, disease and famine ravaged the St. Lawrence. The miserable conditions were made more intolerable by the ostentatious luxury of the unscrupulous, avaricious, and corrupt intendant François Bigot who made his fortune charging outrageous prices to the army for provisions.

Most ominous of all, the ascendancy of William Pitt brought to power in Britain a man determined to rout the French from their overseas strongholds. Using the superior British navy, he designed worldwide attacks on French positions. He sent thousands of regulars to North America for a three-pronged assault on New France, and even guaranteed the colonists payment for equipping their militias! In 1758, the reputedly impregnable fortress at Louisbourg, in fact naked without a protective fleet, fell easily to Jeffrey Amherst. The way was now open for a direct assault on Quebec. The western theater saw the fall of Forts Duquesne and Frontenac in 1758, and thus the collapse of the French position in the West. The Indians there quickly declared neutrality or, much to their future regret, declared for Britain. The Lake Champlain campaign went less well, although the

English regained control of Lake George.

The year 1759 saw James Wolfe's expeditionary force before Quebec. The British ships battered Quebec, and Wolfe sent his American Rangers to terrorize adjacent farmsteads. Yet even now the French position was not hopeless. With the onset of autumn and growing concern about early freezing of the St. Lawrence, Wolfe made his dramatic decision to ascend the cliffs to the Plains of Abraham. A surprised Montcalm foolishly gathered his forces and sent them charging against the British positions. Even the subsequent French defeat might have been avoided if the remaining garrison held out for the arrival of Vaudreuil and the new French commander Lévis. Having captured Quebec, the British were secure only within its walls throughout the winter of 1759–1760. Vaudreuil and Lévis sent desperate requests to Versailles for assistance. In April, 1760 Lévis's troops lured the British to battle outside the walls, and the French victory of Ste.-Foy left the occupiers in a precarious position. However, when the ice thawed it was the British fleet that arrived with reenforcements. Versailles had already conceded defeat in North America.

The British dominance of the seas also brought tangible rewards in the islands. Guadeloupe, Tobago, and Grenada fell in 1759, and after putting up but scant resistance Martinique struck its colors in 1762. Unlike a century earlier in the 1666–67 war, the French colonists did not fiercely resist these conquests, and their capitulation yielded immediate economic rewards. Between 1759 and 1762, Guadeloupe received an influx of twenty thousand slaves and saw an increase in the number of sugar works from 270 to 446. By 1761, the island under British occupation exported three times more sugar than it had in 1755. Even unconquered Saint

Domingue greatly increased its stock of slaves, obviously because of greater opportunities for illicit trade. It was, therefore, with ambivalence that the islanders heard the terms of the Treaty of Paris (1763). The British annexed Tobago, Grenada, St. Vincent, and Dominica but returned the larger sugar islands Martinique and Guadeloupe. The French foreign minister, the Duc de Choiseul (1761–1770), deemed this a great victory; these islands significantly increased the wealth of France while the lost colonies of New France and Louisiana had been a financial albatross. Public opinion in France was, according to Voltaire, indifferent to these colonial losses. He congratulated Choiseul thus: "Permit me to compliment you. I am like the public; I like peace better than Canada and I think France can be happy without Quebec."

CHAPTER VI

Sunset of the Old Regime Empire, 1763–1789

T HE SEVEN YEARS' WAR and the Treaty of Paris have always appeared to subsequent champions of the French colonies as the great debacle. Huge tracts of territory in North America were lost and France's interests in the Indian Ocean seriously impaired. The perfidious British were victorious everywhere, having amply demonstrated how tenuous was the hold of France on her overseas possessions. Nevertheless, from the perspective of France's governing elite, not all had been lost. After all, France retained by far its most valuable colonies, the sugar islands, preserved access to the cod fisheries, and unloaded the financial burden of the North American garrison colonies. To be sure, prevailing mercantilist conceptions demanded that a search be made for colonies to provision the islands, but manifestly New France, and especially Louisiana, had not been realizing that intended purpose anyway.

Even before the Treaty of Paris, the Duc de Choiseul contemplated vengeance on Britain. The keystone to his policy was the maintenance of the Family Compact of 1761, a treaty of friendship between Louis XV and his Bourbon cousin Charles III of Spain.

Choiseul persuaded Spain to join the war against Britain, which resulted, however, in stinging Spanish defeats in the New World, especially the loss of Havana. It was to compensate Spain for her losses — she had to exchange Florida for the return of Havana — that Choiseul ceded western Louisiana (the area west of the Mississippi but including New Orleans). Choiseul's commitment to Spain would be demonstrated again in 1768 when he refused to support a French rebellion in Louisiana against Spanish rule and when he turned over the Falkland (Malouines) Islands to Spanish officials at Argentina.

Close ties with Spain and a naval buildup allowed France to challenge Britain at sea. The number of ships of the line increased from 44 to 66 during Choiseul's ministry. Seeking new naval bases around the world, Choiseul took over Corsica to protect France's Mediterranean fleet and, on the advice of the famous discoverer Bougainville (*Voyage autour du monde*, Paris, 1771) [103], relocated some Acadian families to the strategic Falkland Islands. When war erupted with Britain during the American Revolution, the French fleet won some outstanding

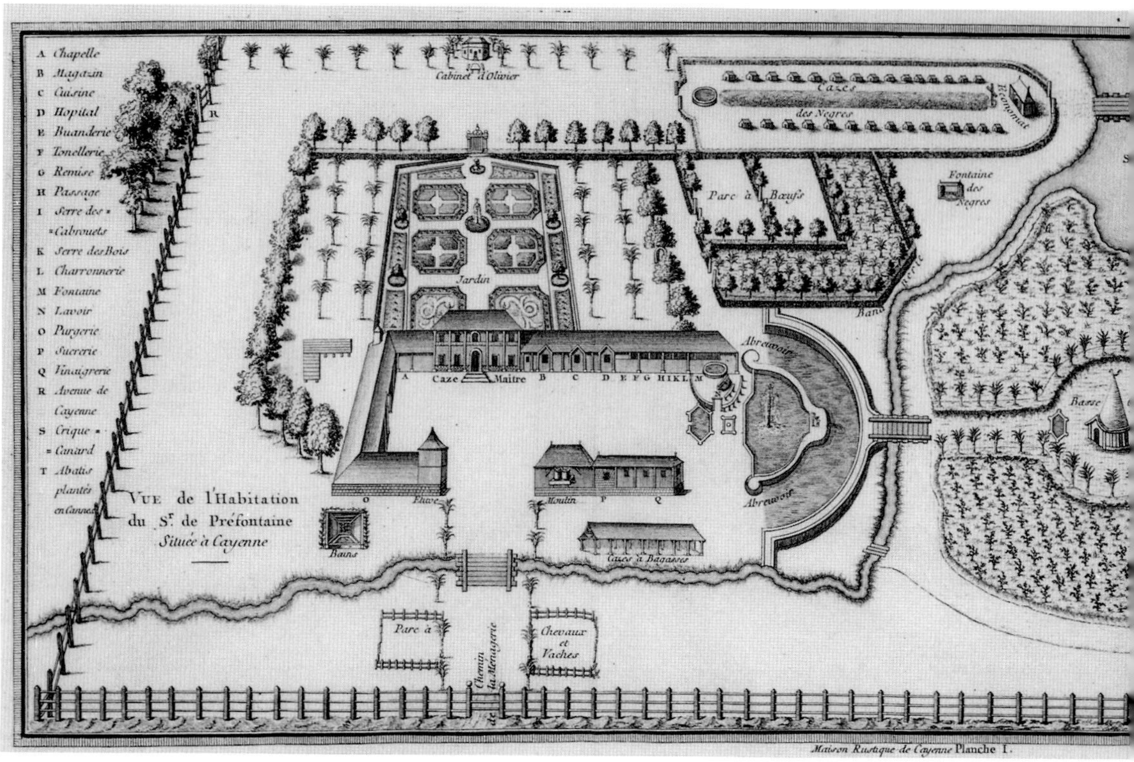
A Chapelle
B Magazin
C Cuisine
D Hopital
E Buanderie
F Tonellerie
G Remise
H Passage
I Serre des Cabrouets
K Serre des Bois
L Charronnerie
M Fontaine
N Lavoir
O Purgerie
P Sucrerie
Q Vinaigrerie
R Avenue de Cayenne
S Crique Canard
T Abatis plantés en Cannes
VUE de l'Habitation du Sr. de Préfontaine Située à Cayenne
Cabinet d'Olivier
Cazes des Negres
Fontaine des Negres
Parc à Bœufs
Jardin
Caze Maitre
Abreuvoir
Moulin
Bains
Cazes à Bagasses
Parc à
Chevaux et Vaches
Chemin de la Menagerie
Maison Rustique de Cayenne Planche I.

Fig. VI.1 "Habitation à Cayenne" from chevalier de Préfontaine, *Maison rustique* (1763).
Préfontaine's plantation at Cayenne. The impressive plantation house and the well-ordered estate were obviously intended to lure potential immigrants.

victories, and as is well known, its blockade at Yorktown in 1781 contributed decisively to the victory that ended the war.

In the long discussions that antedated the signing of the 1763 Treaty of Paris, Choiseul early indicated his willingness to abandon the colonies on the North American continent. He boasted of victory when Britain in effect exchanged Guadeloupe for New France. He agreed to give up east Louisiana (east of the Mississippi) for Ste.-Lucie, an island considered critical to the defense of Martinique and Guadeloupe. Perhaps to rationalize these choices, Choiseul predicted correctly that with the disappearance of the French menace on the mainland, Anglo-Americans would soon revolt against British authority. Throughout the 1760s he sent agents to the British colonies to gauge their support of independence.

The centerpiece of Choiseul's agenda for

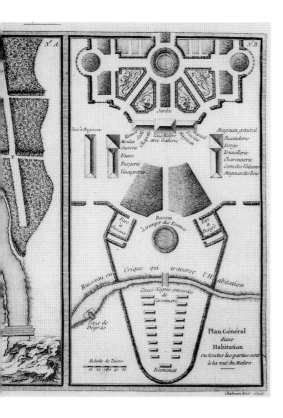

the revival of France's Atlantic empire was the strengthening of the islands. For him, as for all French ministers since Colbert, the valuable Antilles dwarfed in importance all other colonial possessions. To improve island defenses and replace the none-too-zealous militias, Choiseul dispatched professional troops and named military officers as governors. The war hero d'Estaing received such an office at Saint Domingue. These governors were admonished to distance themselves from the planter elites so as to be prepared psychologically to crush their pretensions to independence.

Exactly like Colbert a century before, Choiseul attempted to create a strong French presence at Madagascar and Guiana to control approaches to the Indian Ocean and the Caribbean. Also, vigorous new settlements at Guiana could provision the islands. But Choiseul, unlike Colbert, hoped to establish a predominantly European community at Guiana, because he feared the slave revolts that had ravaged adjacent Dutch Guiana. Also, such a colony could one day provide a strong militia for attacks on Portuguese Brazil. Without knowing much about Guiana other than what he had learned from books and memoirs, Choiseul took vigorous action to promote a colony at the Kourou River. The minister himself was to receive large tracts of land between the Kourou and Marcui rivers, but their value depended on settlement.

The originator of the Kourou project was Bruletout de Préfontaine, a twenty-year veteran of Cayenne, who wanted the government to pump new blood into the anemic colony. To promote the enterprise, he approached the Chevalier de Turgot, brother of the famous physiocrat and later minister, and Thibault de Chanvalon, resident of Martinique and author of the *Voyage à la Martinique* (Paris, 1763) [104]. In 1762, Préfontaine engaged Choiseul in a series of discussions, and the minister was so impressed that he sponsored the publication of Préfontaine's *Maison rustique* (Paris, 1763) [105], a primer for prosperous living at the equator. Dedicated to Choiseul, the book offered the prospective colonist a step-by-step manual for developing a tropical plantation. The author's own successful establishment was empirical proof of what life could be like in Guiana. Préfontaine envisioned the gradual development of Guiana, with immigration to the colony of about two hundred people a year. The minister proved to be far more impatient.

When Préfontaine arrived in Guiana with an advance party, he was astonished to discover that Choiseul, minister of the marine as well as foreign minister, had not instructed officials at Cayenne to support the expedition. The seriousness of this mistake later became dramatically evident. Proceeding to

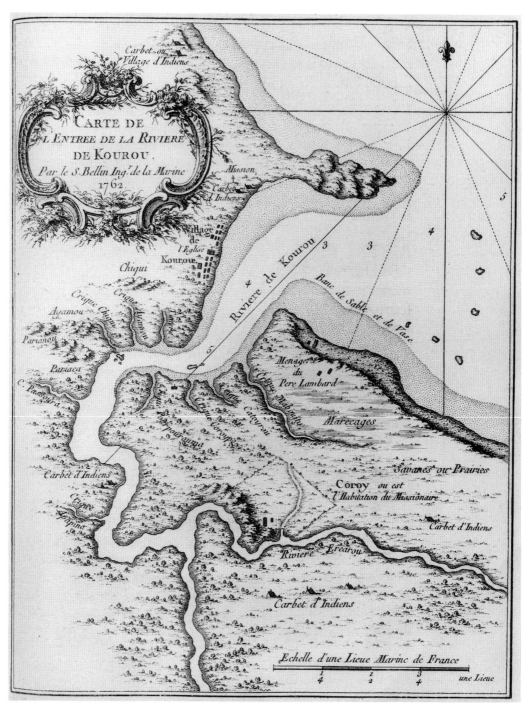

Fig. VI.2 "Entrée de la rivière de Kourou" from Jacques Nicolas Bellin, *Description géographique de la Guiane* (1763). Bellin's map of the lower Kourou River, site of the disastrous colonial expeditions of 1764–65. The Jesuit mission, which helped the new arrivals as much as possible, is on the left bank near the mouth. Bellin clearly depicts the sand banks that so inhibited the landing of supplies.

Kourou, the shaken Préfontaine found the Jesuit mission initially cooperative, and small tracts of land were prepared. Ironically at this time in France, royal *Lettres-patentes* (Lyons, 1763) [106] ordered the seizure of Jesuit property in the colonies.

Meanwhile, an intensive campaign to recruit colonists got under way in France. By order of Choiseul, the marine engineer Bellin published *Description géographique de la Guiane* (Paris, 1763) [107], intended as an all-purpose guide for prospective emigrants. In the same year, M.D.L.S. [Simon Philibert de La Salle de l'Etang] published *Dictionnaire galibi* (Paris) [108]. The author expected that his dictionary would be one of the "principal sources of success" for a new Guiana colony. On a more popular level, promoters inundated Alsace-Lorraine and other areas hard hit by war and taxation with propaganda posters. One of these promised that "the Europeans who emigrate to this beautiful country, which has two harvests per year, will obtain an estate. They will be fed, lodged, well-clothed and furnished with everything they need.... They will not be taxed or bothered about their religious beliefs. Their voyage to Rochefort will be gratis." Drawings of Cayenne festooned with attractive houses and busy cafés flooded eastern France and the Rhineland. Recruiting specifically in areas unfamiliar with Guiana's reputation as a diseased and brutally hot swampland, the promoters had startling success. Of some fifteen thousand colonists who departed in one hundred ships, far and away the largest colonial recruitment in French history, approximately five thousand were Germans and two thousand to three thousand were Alsatians.

What misery these poor recruits were to suffer before some nine thousand died in Guiana and most of the rest straggled back to their homelands! The succession of human errors plaguing this project would be laugh-able were not the cost so dear. The wagon trains of recruits heading for Rochefort and other embarkation ports caused consternation. At Rochefort, as the future governor of Cayenne (then intendant of Rochefort) Pierre-Victor Malouet reported, the authorities were simply unprepared to house and feed the recruits. The leader of the first expedition, Thibault de Chanvalon, and the designated governor-general, Turgot, quarreled. Having received his appointment owing to influence at court, Turgot retired to the comforts of his country estate, leaving Thibault to guide the expedition. On arrival at Cayenne in 1764, the 11 ships and 1,429 colonists received a hostile reception from the royal governor. The expedition, already weakened badly by scurvy and dysentery, sailed west to Kourou where the colonists disembarked before an amazed Préfontaine. The following spring (1764) some fourteen thousand more arrived at a site wracked by malaria, yellow fever, and typhoid, and without adequate housing or food. These colonists, expecting and promised the easy life, refused to work. They ate the available provisions, and sang and danced until disaster struck. When the phlegmatic Turgot was finally roused by Choiseul's ire to assume his command in 1765, he brought to Guiana eight hundred more colonists!

On arrival at Cayenne, Turgot heard reports of the debacle at Kourou and immediately attempted to make Thibault the scapegoat. After ordering the unfortunate intendant home, Turgot himself returned without ever having laid eyes on Kourou. The trial of both men resulted in a life sentence for Thibault (who was later released and compensated after Louis XV died) and exile from Paris for the influential Turgot. Naturally, the person who bore the ultimate responsibility, Choiseul, continued as minister.

Coming so soon after the dismantling of

the French colonial empire at the Treaty of Paris, the disaster at Kourou further damaged pro-colonial sentiment in France. Thousands of lives were needlessly lost and thirty million *livres* vanished. Within a few decades, politicians of the French Revolution would cast their eyes on Guiana as an appropriate site for a penal colony.

Between the disaster at Kourou and the establishment of a penal colony, Guiana made some perceptible gains. Some two hundred families of the Kourou expedition survived and set down roots. The population climbed from about 666 whites and 4,600 blacks in 1740 to 1,735 whites and 10,475 blacks in 1789. Oddly, the fiasco at Kourou failed to deter some of its organizers, who blamed inadequate leadership. Choiseul himself became involved in a proposed settlement on the Tonnegrande River in 1767, and another eight hundred thousand *livres* disappeared. In 1776, the Baron de Bessner, previously in charge of the Kourou promotional campaign and then associated with Choiseul in the Tonnegrande project, proposed the amazing scheme of transporting some two hundred members of the suppressed Jesuit order to Guiana. Large numbers of Indians and escaped blacks were to be rounded up and placed under Jesuit control, and it was hoped that another Paraguay would be the result. Bessner and his associates were to split the profits with the Jesuits.

The arrival of Malouet as governor in 1776 not only permits a look at Cayenne's squalid conditions but demonstrates the intractability of the colony's problems. An enlightened bureaucrat, Malouet discussed in his memoirs his vigorous efforts to overcome the lethargy of Cayenne's inhabitants who were almost all severely indebted to the king and French merchants. Few ships visited Cayenne, and the planters produced sugar almost exclusively for the local rum trade. The energetic Malouet tried unsuc-

cessfully to forbid the sale of rum. He traveled to Suriname to study the secrets of the Dutch success there, and he brought back an engineer to show the colonists how to drain their swamps. But the colonists apparently had little interest in the engineer or in their meddling governor, who sailed home in frustration in 1778.

While Malouet was in Cayenne, the experienced surgeon Bajon published *Mémoires... de Cayenne* (Paris, 1777) [109]. Dedicated to the new minister of the marine, Sartine, this book once more sought to dispel the negative public image of Guiana. It was not disease and climate that blocked progress at Cayenne but the colonists' indulgent behavior in matters of food, liquor, and sex. Frenchmen could live well in the tropics if they adjusted their appetites to nature's imperatives. A decade later, M. Guisan in his *Traité, sur... Guiane* (Cayenne, 1788) [110] also prescribed remedies for improving living conditions there. Clearly, some Frenchmen had not abandoned hope for the colony.

It is clear from a simple survey of French publications about America in the period after 1763 that her colonial losses did not extinguish France's interest in the New World. In fact, never before had the Americas attracted such public attention, and appropriately so. In bald economic terms, the years between 1763 and 1789 were the most productive of the old colonial empire. The islands, particularly Saint Domingue, generated wealth for France far outstripping any previous period, as is easily demonstrated by a few statistics. Not only did Saint Domingue double its sugar production, but its "coffee revolution" increased production from seven million pounds in 1755 to seventy-seven million in 1789. These figures represented about forty percent of the world's sugar at the time and more than half of its coffee. A corresponding increase in slave imports fueled this boom. The number of

Fig. VI.3 "L'Isle St. Domingue" from Moreau de Saint-Méry, *Description topographique et politique de la partie espagnole de l'isle Saint-Domingue* (1796). This map clearly shows the French part of Hispaniola, then known as Saint-Domingue, today as Haiti. Moreau also demarcates the three administrative divisions of this richest eighteenth-century colony.

slaves in Saint Domingue roughly doubled to 480,000 between 1774 and 1790. All in all, some 677 French ships serviced the islands in 1788 compared with about 100 a century earlier. The French Antilles had become the richest colonies in the world.

In the aftermath of the serious defeats of the Seven Years' War, Versailles introduced several reforms to strengthen royal authority in the islands and to discipline colonists who had displayed less than heroic conduct during that struggle. Colonial governors were given the command of regular troops, which permitted the disbandment of island militias. The administration first extracted four million *livres* from the colonists as a substitute for militia duty; then later Versailles reimposed the militia. The official desire to put these upstart colonists in their place was analogous to Whitehall's view of Anglo-Americans; and the angry whites of Saint Domingue responded similarly.

The French government attempted in 1763 to reestablish the *Exclusif* after nearly twenty years of exceptions and "emergencies." The only concession was the establishment of a free port at Môle St. Nicholas in Saint Domingue; there wood could be exchanged for *tafia* and rum. In 1769, Ste.-Lucie was permitted to serve the same function in the Lesser Antilles. Over time these slight cracks in the *Exclusif* widened.

The islanders, whose rebellious roots reached back to their founding fathers, responded vigorously to these government "reforms." When d'Estaing attempted to integrate mulattoes into the Saint Domingue militia, white dissent was so vociferous that the project was shelved and d'Estaing recalled (1765). Mulattoes were instead allowed to form "colored" militias, with important consequences for the revolutionary 1790s. Three years after d'Estaing's departure, colonists in the southern and western provinces of Saint Domingue took up arms against efforts to enforce the *Exclusif*. A remarkable development in this affair was that Governor Rohan promised mulattoes equal treatment in return for military assistance against the rebels.

Published between 1776 and 1777, the *Considérations sur . . . Saint Domingue* (Paris) [111] by Hilliard d'Auberteuil represented well the Saint Domingue colonists' resentment of the mercantilist state. Employing the fashionable terminology of social contracts between governors and governed to protect humanity and justice, the author invoked the principle of utility as the primary justification of the colonial relationship; it was legitimate only as long as each side was useful to the other. The book made clear how useful Saint Domingue was to France, but it insisted that her value could not continue without contraband slaves. The *Exclusif* was not only unjust, it was also impractical because competition and island self-interest would always defeat it. Finally, the book severely criticized metropolitan policies that resulted in the loss of Louisiana and New France. Not surprisingly, an *Arrêt du Conseil d'Etat du roi* (Paris, 1777) [112] banned the book.

Unlike the case of the English colonies on the North American continent, these island upheavals did not mushroom into full-scale rebellions. Resentment against the *Exclusif* was mitigated somewhat during the American War for Independence when island ports were opened to the Americans' shipping. Also, the strength of French naval forces in the Caribbean put the government in an advantageous position. Nevertheless, after the Treaty of Paris (1783), Louis XVI and the minister of the marine, the Duc de Castries, opened five more ports for limited trade with foreigners. Even so, these breaches in the *Exclusif* excluded American flour and were accompanied by a crackdown on smuggling, which meant higher prices for slaves.

The port openings moderately pleased island whites, but deteriorating racial conditions at home and the growing volume of abolitionist criticism in France boded ill for the future. At Saint Domingue, the "insolence" of the growing numbers of mulattoes, who would in 1789 roughly equal the number of whites (about 30,000), exacerbated social tensions. Local superior councils responded with a variety of "apartheid" measures. *Petits blancs*, whose numbers doubled between 1765 and 1789, especially resented the upwardly mobile "browns," many of whom had prospered during the "coffee revolution." Royal officials generally supported these racist measures, perhaps to prevent any alliance between white and mulatto planters. At the same time, in all the islands, but especially Saint Domingue, a flood of Africans poured in to feed the monstrous plantation system. The 270,000 African imports in the 1780s equalled the total number of imports of the previous three decades, and by 1789 blacks would outnumber whites at Saint Domingue by more than six to one.

Under increasing pressure from enlightened opinion at home, Versailles attempted to reinvigorate previous slave codes that protected blacks from abuse. In 1777 Hilliard d'Auberteuil [111] had frankly admitted that importation of some 800,000 Africans since 1680 had produced a black population of only 290,000. The author attributed this human tragedy to the tyranny of white masters, and called for reforms to encourage black family formation. But the sensational Le Jeune case, in which a superior council blatantly infringed the Black Code by pardoning Le Jeune for torturing six of his slaves to death, exemplified Saint Domingue's response to criticism.

The emergence in France of public debate about colonial slavery produced greater intransigence in the islands. In his one month tenure as minister of the marine, A.R.J. Turgot in 1774 called for the substitution of free labor. After succeeding Turgot on Louis XV's death, Sartine asked Malouet to respond to the famed economist. Malouet circulated in manuscript the book later published as *Mémoire sur l'esclavage des nègres* (Neuchâtel, 1788) [113]. He articulated what would long be the official view of slavery as a necessary evil that should be rendered more tolerable by vigorous enforcement of protective laws. These views drew a strong response from the humanitarian Condorcet, alias Pasteur Schwartz, *Réflexions sur l'esclavage des nègres* (Neuchâtel, 1781) [114]. A third position, the unabashedly proslavery argument, appeared in, among other works, Dubuisson's *Nouvelles considérations sur Saint-Domingue* (Paris, 1780) [115], a rebuttal of d'Auberteuil's call for reforms in the treatment of slaves. In 1785, the Abbé Raynal's *Essai sur l'administration de St. Domingue*

([Geneva]) [116] presented once more the official, pragmatic defense of slavery. This author, so famous for his radical *Histoire... des Européens dans les deux Indes* (Geneva, 1780) [117] which attacked slavery, now argued that although slavery was a fundamental violation of human rights, were not Africans better off living in a progressive civilization? Only switching the word "Christian" for "progressive" demonstrates the persistence of a four-hundred-year-old justification. In 1789, Brissot de Warville entered the fray on the side of Condorcet with his *Mémoire sur les noirs de l'Amérique septentrionale* (Paris) [118], in which he called for the establishment of an abolitionist society in Paris to cooperate with that of London.

Two important books about Saint Domingue during the Old Regime were published in 1796–1797, and the tumult of the Revolutionary 1790s inevitably colored their perspectives and interpretations. An émigré living in Philadelphia, Moreau de Saint-Méry wrote a massively detailed apology for the plantation system entitled *Description... de l'isle Saint-Domingue* (Philadelphia, 1796) [119]. Like others of his class, Moreau strongly argued that only Africans could perform hard, physical labor in the climate of the islands, and he devoted many pages to rationalizing their particular fitness for slavery. In another major publication a year later Baron de Wimpffen reported on his travels in Saint Domingue during those crucial years, 1788 to 1790, in *Voyage à Saint-Domingue* (Paris, 1797) [120]. Critical of planter society and especially of white refusal to acknowledge the worth of prosperous mulattoes, he contradicted Moreau de Saint-Méry [119] about the race and labor connection. Whites could work in the coffee industry, for example. Wimpffen attacked both the horrors of the slave trade and the utopianism of abolitionists who failed to explain how sugar could be produced without slaves. Analyzing the roots of revolution in the islands, he blamed white resistance to royal authority on habits formed as slave-masters. These habits accustomed them to exercise authoritarian, even tyrannical, methods on their estates; but he also blamed the corruption of royal officials for colonial resistance in the late 1780s.

The approach of the French Revolution found the islands in a troubled state. Planter challenges to a royal administration intent on reform increased. While slaves were gen-

erally quiet, the proverbial peace before the storm, mulattoes displayed increasing resentment at their unequal treatment. Their representatives in Paris supported the creation of the celebrated *Société des Amis des Noirs* (Society of Friends of the Blacks). In turn, such tidings from France fed paranoia among the island whites, especially the *petits blancs*. It would take but the spark of revolution in France to light the powder keg in the Antilles.

France may have evacuated the North

Fig. VI.4 On the distinction of color, from Alexandre-Stanislas, baron de Wimpffen, *Voyage à Saint-Domingue* (1797). Wimpffen discusses here the power of color prejudice at Saint-Domingue. Even if, he writes, a Negro could prove descent from the black Magus and could demonstrate the highest genius, he would still be scorned by the most impoverished white colonial.

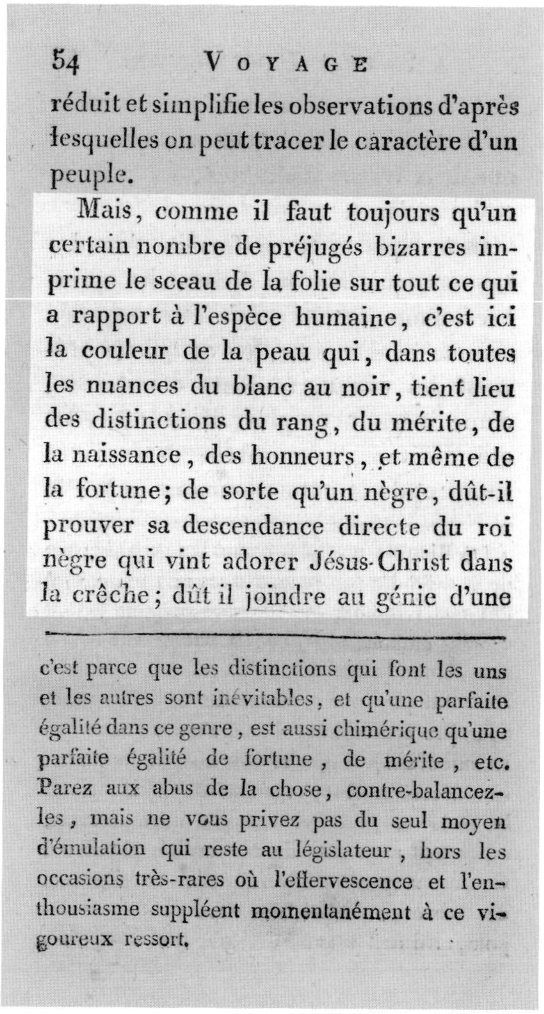

54   VOYAGE

réduit et simplifie les observations d'après lesquelles on peut tracer le caractère d'un peuple.

Mais, comme il faut toujours qu'un certain nombre de préjugés bizarres imprime le sceau de la folie sur tout ce qui a rapport à l'espèce humaine, c'est ici la couleur de la peau qui, dans toutes les nuances du blanc au noir, tient lieu des distinctions du rang, du mérite, de la naissance, des honneurs, et même de la fortune; de sorte qu'un nègre, dût-il prouver sa descendance directe du roi nègre qui vint adorer Jésus-Christ dans la crèche; dût il joindre au génie d'une

c'est parce que les distinctions qui font les uns et les autres sont inévitables, et qu'une parfaite égalité dans ce genre, est aussi chimérique qu'une parfaite égalité de fortune, de mérite, etc. Parez aux abus de la chose, contre-balancez-les, mais ne vous privez pas du seul moyen d'émulation qui reste au législateur, hors les occasions très-rares où l'effervescence et l'enthousiasme suppléent momentanément à ce vigoureux ressort.

American continent in 1763, but events there continued to elicit much interest. In Louisiana, what should have been an orderly transfer of power to Spanish rule was instead a debacle. Versailles ordered French officials at New Orleans to cooperate with the Spanish, but the first Spanish governor, Don Antonio de Ulloa, arrived without troops. For more than two years he ruled through the former French governor. However, when Ulloa attempted to impose mercantilist restrictions *à l'espagnole,* a conspiracy developed against him. The rebels first looked to the English at Mobile for support, then made their case to Choiseul. The minister hesitated briefly, but in the end the Family Compact proved too vital to jeopardize by meddling in Louisiana. Moreover, as no significant mercantile constituency in France depended on Louisiana, little political pressure could be applied to Choiseul. Therefore, when in 1768 the Spanish sent troops under Alejandro O'Reilly to restore control, Choiseul did not act except to encourage leniency for the rebels. A good account of this affair, which is favorable to the French rebels, appears in Jean Bernard Bossu's second, expanded edition of the *Nouveaux voyages dans l'Amérique septentrionale* (Amsterdam, 1777) [**121**]. In 1773, Colonel Champigny published his *La Louisiane ensanglantée* in London [**122**] to recommend the Louisiana French to Britain in case of war with Spain. A hater of Spain and bitter about Louis XV's abandonment of Louisiana, Champigny made heroes of the rebels and published their long testament justifying their conduct.

After the failure of the 1768 rebellion, French settlers resigned themselves to Spanish rule. Further north up the Mississippi, many settlers on the east side of the river crossed to the west preferring Spanish to English rule. Older west-bank settlements like Sainte Genevieve and newly founded communities like Saint Louis prospered during the half-century before the Louisiana purchase (1803). Fur traders and explorers based at Saint Louis pushed up the Missouri out to the Rockies.

The initial Canadian bitterness about France's abandonment of New France receded gradually after 1763. As large numbers of notables departed in 1760–1763, British "peddlers" descended upon Montreal and Quebec to take over the fur trade. However, a succession of competent British governors prevented their countrymen from plundering the conquered country. Accommodations were made, among the most important being the expedient tolerance of the Catholic Church. The famous Quebec Act of 1774, which was anathema in the thirteen British colonies that later became the U.S., was another example of imperial pragmatism, designed to placate the *Canadiens*. In turn, *habitants* generally, if unenthusiastically, cooperated with the British. The Catholic Church in France ordered its priests to stay in Canada. At Quebec, people like François Cugnet compiled volumes of old French laws and customs to inform the new rulers (*Traité de la police*, Quebec, 1775) [**123**]. It is not surprising that French Canadians did not take advantage of British vulnerability during the American Revolution. The War of American Independence had nothing to do with Canadians. Few aided the British to defend the colony from American invasion and even fewer assisted the rebel forces that captured Montreal and besieged Quebec. Even when France recognized the rebels and forged an alliance with them in 1778, the *Canadiens* were not stirred; and rightly so because the French foreign minister, the Comte de Vergennes, expressed no interest in reclaiming the colony.

If neither Louisiana nor Canada aroused the enthusiasm of old France, the new American Republic did. To be sure, initial French support for the American rebels grew out of traditional power politics and the aching for *revanche* for the losses of 1763. Vergennes, who as early as 1763 had predicted a colonial revolt against Britain, began providing covert aid to the Americans in 1776. However, as young aristocratic officers volunteered to help the rebels, support for the American cause often became as much an ideological statement as a political one, liberty being the announced aim rather than reason-of-state. Even after American rude treatment of France at the Treaty of Paris (1783), the French government and people continued to strongly support the new republic. Louis XVI in 1787 granted most-favored-nation status to Americans, a rare privilege in those days. (See the *Arrêt du Conseil d'Etat du roi*, Paris, 1788) [**124**]. Many literary works of the 1780s reflected this sympathetic approach. Abbé Robin's *Nouveau voyage* (Paris and Philadelphia, 1782) [**125**], which described the friendly reception of Rochambeau's army as it marched from Newport to Yorktown, and M. de Chastellux's *Voyage...en Amérique*

([Paris], 1785) [**126**], which recounts extensive discussions with Thomas Jefferson on such issues as democracy and slavery, are but two examples.

The amazing popularity of America in France after 1776 provided an opportunity for numerous writers to attack the well-entrenched opinion that America was an inherently inferior environment. In the great "Dispute of the New World," influential works of the respected French botanist Buffon and the Dutch-born Cornelius De Pauw argued that animal forms and man degenerated in the New World environment uncontrolled by the hand of civilized man. Not only were Amerindians primitive, but European migrants to the New World had produced nothing intellectually of any import. Of the many who rushed to America's defense in the 1780s were Filippo Mazzei in *Recherches historiques et politiques sur les Etats-Unis de l'Amérique septentrionale* (Colle and Paris, 1788) [**127**] and G.R. Carli in *Lettres américaines* (Boston and Paris, 1788) [**128**].

CHAPTER VII

Revolution and the Last Crisis, 1789–1815

THE GREAT FRENCH REVOLUTION of 1789 had a dramatic impact on France's colonies in America. If by 1815 France retained Guiana, Martinique, and Guadeloupe, she no longer drew wealth from fabulous Saint Domingue, which was now Haiti under black control. And under Napoleon the *métropole* had regained title to Louisiana but failed to occupy and develop the North American interior. Once again, it was France's European interests and her naval inferiority to Britain that dictated a further weakening of her American connection.

Two years of economic and political crises preceded the outbreak of the Revolution. At home and in the colonies, royal officials struggled to maintain control. Stung by aristocratic-led turmoil that foiled its efforts to overcome budget deficits, Louis XVI's government nevertheless attempted to address colonial problems. It renewed efforts to protect slaves, to prevent smuggling, and to reform colonial finances. But unrest was percolating, especially at Saint Domingue, and when in 1788 Louis XVI called for elections for an estates-general, colonial dissidents rushed to take advantage of the opportunity this presented. Whites in the

islands had been outraged by official decrees attempting to restrict masters' control of their slaves. Inspired by the example of the French parlements, the *Conseil Supérieur* at Le Cap François, Saint Domingue, refused to register such edicts; in fact, these "tyrannical" decrees were as ineffective as they were irritating. The planters of course saw an additional advantage in the upheavals: the weakening of the *Exclusif*.

These two years of troubles also excited the hopes of the islands' increasingly numerous and prosperous mulattoes. They were particularly strong in the west and south provinces of Saint Domingue, where they outnumbered whites. Beyond their economic successes—and they claimed to own more than one quarter of the land and slaves at Saint Domingue—mulattoes yearned for social respect and political equality. Scorned by even the poorest white and laughed at by the darkest slave, they naturally responded to the slogan "Liberty, Equality, Fraternity" emanating from France.

As for the slaves, little can be known about their response to rumors of revolution in France. Despite booming numbers of African imports in the 1780s, and, according to many accounts, increasingly brutal exploitation, the years before the black rebellion of 1791 were quiet. The rate of *marronage* remained steady; the number of conspiracies was negligible; even the fad of poisoning other slaves became rarer. The opening of the American trade after 1784 guaranteed minimum supplies of food for the slaves. Tensions within slave ranks also worked to prevent overt resistance to the white regime. Creoles (i.e., the American-born) scorned newly arrived "saltwater" blacks. Tribal members carried their hatreds across the Atlantic. Only with the outbreak of the French Revolution and with their masters breaking the chains of metropolitan dominance would the slaves seize the opportunity to strike for their freedom. As Toussaint Louverture, later leader of the black cause, said: "They tolerated their chains as long as they knew no state happier than slavery."

In the Antilles in 1789, the enormous social hatreds within and among racial groups were mitigated neither by old-fashioned shared religious values nor the modern tonic of nationalism. When the Revolution erupted in France, its message inundated the islands with a tidal wave of liberty. However, in the colonies *liberté* meant very different things to different classes and racial groups.

After the fall of the Bastille on July 14, 1789, which marked the victory of the popular revolution in France, whites at Saint Domingue moved to nullify royal rule. The hated intendant Barbé-Marbois was sent packing, and soon the government recalled the powerless Governor Chilleau. After these triumphs, whites divided along socioeconomic lines and fought for political ascendancy. Some remained loyal to royal government and opposed to the Revolution; all wanted effective legislative independence, but each faction vied for control of the legislature. The north province, that with the strongest royalist sentiment, fought the

west dominated by *Patriotes*, whose name indicated their confraternity with the revolutionaries of 1789. *Grands blancs* generally wanted greater autonomy from France without social revolution. *Petits blancs*, although many served whatever group paid them, generally sympathized with the *Patriotes*, a faction that included some planters and middle-class elements.

Traditional hatred of the *Exclusif* and growing concern with France's perceived "softness" on the color issue fueled the colonists' drive to greater autonomy, if not independence. Frustrated in their efforts to be heard in the islands, the mulattoes exerted pressure on the French National Assembly (1789–1791) to have their "Rights of Man" recognized. They joined forces with the *Société des Amis des Noirs*. The Abbé Grégoire's *Mémoire en faveur des gens de couleur* (Paris, 1789) [129], which detailed the prejudices against island mulattoes, is just one of the *Société's* tracts held by the John Carter Brown Library. Mulatto efforts, however, had little impact on the French National Assembly and its Committee on the Colonies. For two years, white absentee planters in France in conjunction with the powerful colonial trade interests were able to table any legislation on behalf of mulattoes. In effect, planter interests fashioned a bargain with mercantile interests to dominate the Committee on Colonies. The planters received assurance of autonomy in race relations, and the mercantile interests received planter assurance that the *Exclusif* would remain intact.

The situation in the islands deteriorated in 1790: civil war broke out at Martinique, and an independent assembly at Saint Marc, Saint Domingue opened all ports to foreign commerce. Furthermore, the brutal suppression of a mulatto rising, followed by the execution of its leader, Ogé, polarized Saint Domingue. In France, the colonial deputies in the National Assembly aggravated public opinion by their taunting denials of France's right to have any say whatsoever in the colonies' internal affairs; revolution in the colonies, they boldly asserted in 1791, would be the response to such interference. In May of 1791 the National Assembly passed a very moderate resolution calling for full citizenship for mulattoes born of two free parents. Although only a tiny minority of mulattoes would benefit from this resolution, white islanders balked at implementing it. In frustration, the mulattoes of Saint Domingue revolted in the summer of 1791 and started the chain of events leading to the demise of the French regime. A good survey of the history of white-mulatto conflicts at Saint Domingue can be found in the *Mémoire sur les causes des troubles…de Saint-Domingue* (Paris, 1793) [130] by J. Raimond, the leader of the mulatto cause in France.

By their recalcitrant opposition to even moderate alterations of mulatto status, white islanders fostered conditions favorable to the slave revolt that broke out in the northern plains in August 1791. Such at least was the thesis offered by Garran-Coulon in his exhaustive and official *Rapport sur les troubles de Saint-Domingue* (Paris, 1797–1799) [131]. It should, nevertheless, be emphasized that the slave revolts occurred within the context of the white-mulatto struggle. In the north, mulattoes apparently cooperated with the black rebels, whereas in the south and west whites incited the slaves to turn against the numerous and powerful mulattoes. Quite apparently, royal officials, whites, and mulattoes all saw potential advantage in manipulating the slave rebels, and those conflicting calculations prevented the suppression of the black revolution.

One of the early leaders of the slave rebellion was Toussaint, later Toussaint Louverture after he came to dominate the black liberation movement. A trusted and privileged slave who achieved freedom as early as the 1770s, the devoutly Catholic Toussaint only slowly came to support liberty for all slaves and even then within the context of the plantation system. In the early years of the upheaval, apparently most blacks in revolt would and occasionally did accept improved conditions on the plantations in return for putting down their arms. Only in 1793 did the demands of black leaders include freedom, and even then only for their fighters. In short, the white and brown elites had two years to resolve their disputes before they lost control of the black rebels.

In early 1792, conditions at Saint Domingue stabilized somewhat when the Legislative Assembly (1791–1792) in France decreed equality for mulattoes. Although resisted by many whites, this measure and the arrival of troops from France brought about a gradual restoration of peace. But not for long. Changes in revolutionary France once again drove forward the Saint Domingue revolution. After the overthrow of the monarchy and the birth of the First French Republic (Aug. – Sept. 1792), the civil commissioners Sonthonax and Polverel arrived to restore order and implement decrees granting mulatto equality. Their pro-mulatto policies alienated many whites, who ironically now looked with growing sympathy toward the deposed Louis XVI. But then in France, too, many "liberal" nobles were undergoing the same transformation.

In the Lesser Antilles, royal governors led Martinique and Guadeloupe into counterrevolution on news of the abolition of the monarchy. Soon, however, the Republic's naval forces allowed her commissioners to join forces with the *Patriotes*. But continuing social and political strife within these islands opened the way for a British takeover of Guadeloupe and Martinique. In 1794, however, the energetic Republican commissioner Victor Hugues led a campaign to reconquer

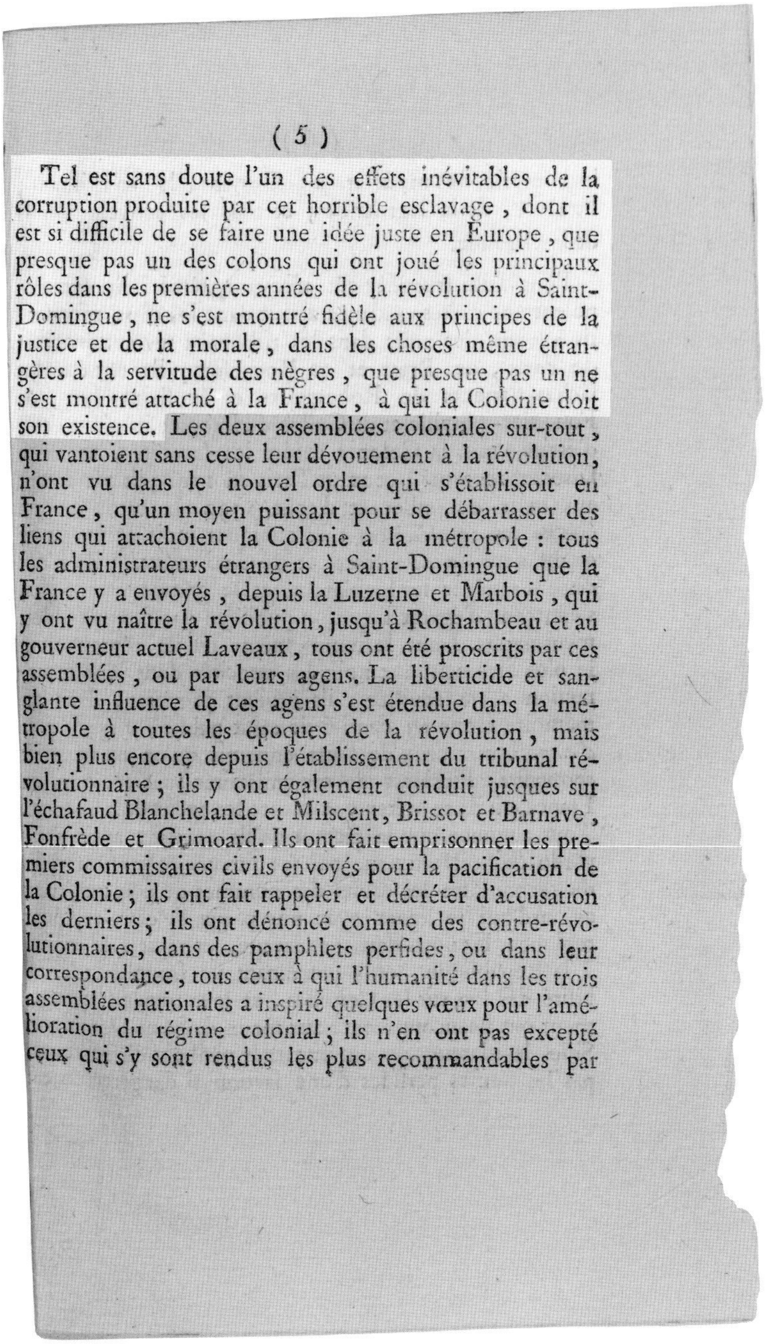

(5)

Tel est sans doute l'un des effets inévitables de la corruption produite par cet horrible esclavage, dont il est si difficile de se faire une idée juste en Europe, que presque pas un des colons qui ont joué les principaux rôles dans les premières années de la révolution à Saint-Domingue, ne s'est montré fidèle aux principes de la justice et de la morale, dans les choses même étrangères à la servitude des nègres, que presque pas un ne s'est montré attaché à la France, à qui la Colonie doit son existence. Les deux assemblées coloniales sur-tout, qui vantoient sans cesse leur dévouement à la révolution, n'ont vu dans le nouvel ordre qui s'établissoit en France, qu'un moyen puissant pour se débarrasser des liens qui attachoient la Colonie à la métropole : tous les administrateurs étrangers à Saint-Domingue que la France y a envoyés, depuis la Luzerne et Marbois, qui y ont vu naître la révolution, jusqu'à Rochambeau et au gouverneur actuel Laveaux, tous ont été proscrits par ces assemblées, ou par leurs agens. La liberticide et sanglante influence de ces agens s'est étendue dans la métropole à toutes les époques de la révolution, mais bien plus encore depuis l'établissement du tribunal révolutionnaire ; ils y ont également conduit jusques sur l'échafaud Blanchelande et Milscent, Brissot et Barnave, Fonfrède et Grimoard. Ils ont fait emprisonner les premiers commissaires civils envoyés pour la pacification de la Colonie ; ils ont fait rappeler et décréter d'accusation les derniers ; ils ont dénoncé comme des contre-révolutionnaires, dans des pamphlets perfides, ou dans leur correspondance, tous ceux à qui l'humanité dans les trois assemblées nationales a inspiré quelques vœux pour l'amélioration du régime colonial ; ils n'en ont pas excepté ceux qui s'y sont rendus les plus recommandables par

Fig. VII.1 Page from *Rapport sur les troubles de Saint-Domingue* (1797–1799).
In this official report, the author blames the corruption inevitably fostered by the slave system as the cause of planter infidelity to France. The hostility of the white colonists at Saint-Domingue to the French Revolution and its agents was rooted in their hope for independence, according to Garran.

Guadeloupe. Subsequently Hugues had to impose dictatorship to keep order in this badly fragmented colony.

Dramatic events in France and Saint Domingue characterized the years after 1793. In that year, France and Britain went to war. In a short period, the British took the great naval base at Toulon, captured Guadeloupe, Martinique, and Ste.-Lucie, and at the behest of some planters invaded the south and west of Saint Domingue. As in earlier conflicts, the Antilles were vulnerable to British naval actions. With the French Republic at its low ebb in 1793, Sonthonax took the desperate expedient of arming slaves against their masters in the north of Saint Domingue, and in August he declared general emancipation. Frightened whites, especially the planters, and even some mulattoes broke all ties with France to support British occupation forces. Meanwhile Spain, also at war with the French Republic, invaded Saint Domingue from Santo Domingo, and her forces attracted black rebels including Toussaint with promises of freedom. These black fighters simply did not believe the Republic would legitimize Sonthonax's proclamation and, in any case, the revolution in France appeared to be in its death throes.

The French Republic revived dramatically in 1794 under Robespierre and the Committee of Public Safety, and its reinvigorated armies swept the Prussians and Austrians from national soil. In the Caribbean, Republican forces ejected the British from Guadeloupe and raised rebellions in some minor English islands. When the Republic abolished slavery in February, news of this dramatic event induced black rebels to join Republican forces. Toussaint abandoned the Spanish in May. Soon the British and Spanish forces, which had refused to cooperate, were contained, and troops under the French Republican General Laveaux and Toussaint scored some smashing victories. Debilitated by yellow fever, the British army became so weak that it also used the expedient of offering freedom for slaves who would fight for it.

In 1795, Spain withdrew from the coalition fighting France and ceded Santo Domingo. The following year Britain threw significant new forces into Saint Domingue, but soon disease along with poor planning and poor leadership neutralized this temporary advantage. The Republican forces could not take advantage of their opportunities because of internecine rivalries. Most troubling were the mulattoes, disgusted by Laveaux's favoring of Toussaint's forces. After squelching a mulatto coup at Le Cap in 1796, Toussaint became deputy governor. The Republican cause increasingly depended on the loyalty of the black leader.

Republican forces under Toussaint in the north and the mulatto leader Rigaud in the south made significant headway in 1797 against British and planter forces in the occupied zone. In fact, the British had abandoned hope of anything more than using their positions in Saint Domingue as a bargaining chip at the peace treaty. Many of the remaining whites now despaired and joined their fellow émigrés in London, Philadelphia, and elsewhere. Sonthonax, having returned in 1796, named Toussaint as governor. Backed by a growing and more seasoned army, Toussaint eliminated all rivals in the north and even evicted Sonthonax. Only Rigaud remained a contestant for control of republican Saint Domingue. But first, in 1798, the two leaders united for a final drive on crumbling British positions. Many of the blacks in the British army deserted to Toussaint. In May, the British withdrew from the west following Toussaint's guarantee of protection for the remaining whites. The typically conciliatory but also shrewd Toussaint wanted to maintain trade connections with Britain.

The republic sent out General Hédouville as its new representative in 1798. His sole source of power, however, was his ability to set mulattoes against blacks and Toussaint succeeded in expelling him quickly. When the remaining French Commissioner, Roume, proposed in 1799 to invade Jamaica, Toussaint undermined him by revealing the plans to the British. In the same year Toussaint invaded the south and defeated Rigaud, which made it quite clear who was in control of Saint Domingue. In 1800 Toussaint invaded and quickly captured Santo Domingo.

Toussaint Louverture now embarked on the reconstruction of the island. He reestablished the plantation system based on forced but nonslave labor. Many former plantation owners were invited to return to their properties. On these estates, one-fourth of the profits went to the workers, one-fourth to the owner, and one-half to the state. The army and its commander enforced a paternalistic discipline on the freedmen. Toussaint complemented this policy by opening Saint Domingue to all shippers; in fact, he had had close ties with the "Bostonians" for a number of years. Furthermore, he guaranteed noninterference in adjacent slave islands. This basically conservative revolutionary wanted a multiracial society cooperating under the watchful eyes of a paternalistic military.

There was by this time a military ruler in France as well. Napoleon Bonaparte also promoted a solution to revolutionary anarchy that combined military dictatorship and egalitarian rhetoric; thus, Toussaint was a "Bonapartist" even before the Corsican himself. Bonaparte planned to restore order in France as a prelude to power beyond her frontiers. The peace of Amiens in 1802 with Britain allowed Napoleon to implement plans for a restoration of France's American empire.

What was the overall picture in the colonies after a decade of turmoil? For Guiana, one of near anarchy. By 1789 blacks outnumbered whites nearly ten to one. Before the abolition of slavery in 1794, there was much tension between masters and slaves, some brawls, and some burning of plantations. With the end of slavery, blacks left the plantations to establish small farms. All of these events were of little concern to the French Republic, which looked upon Guiana as a dumping ground for political prisoners. The numbers deported increased sharply after the overthrow of the Committee of Public Safety in 1794 and public revulsion against the guillotine. Guiana became the "dry guillotine" because most prisoners died there before release. Accounts of this ordeal by escapees further blackened Guiana's reputation. After his ascent to power, Napoleon sent the veteran colonial official Victor Hugues to Cayenne with plans to restore slavery, but little was accomplished before Guiana fell to the Portuguese.

By 1799, only Guadeloupe and Saint Domingue remained under nominal French rule. The British, reversing earlier losses, had again occupied Martinique, Ste.-Lucie, Tobago, and other small islands. The Revolution had nakedly exposed the raw social and racial conflicts of the islands. Many whites had emigrated, some ten thousand from Saint Domingue alone. As a result of both ideology and expediency the Republic had abolished slavery which, combined with British blockades, had radically decreased island trade with France. It was evident to Napoleon and the mercantile interests so harmed by these developments that restoration of *métropole* control and of slavery was vital to France's economic future. An expedition would have to be sent to Saint Domingue to remove Toussaint who, much to Bonaparte's chagrin, labeled himself the "Black Napoleon."

Although the key to Bonaparte's colonial policy was control of the sugar islands, he also had designs on the North American continent. Canada, to be sure, little interested him, and in any case its French-speaking peoples had shown little enthusiasm at the events of 1789 and even less as the Revolution attacked Church and Crown. But Louisiana had great potential as both an economic and a strategic base. A strong French colony there would slow down the American advance to the west and put pressure on the new republic to maintain friendship with France. A populous Louisiana would also provide the manpower to threaten Mexico in case of war against Spain. Economically, Louisiana could supply essential provisions such as timber, cattle, and wheat to the islands. None of these arguments was new.

Napoleon's successful campaign to force Spain to retrocede Louisiana was the culmi-

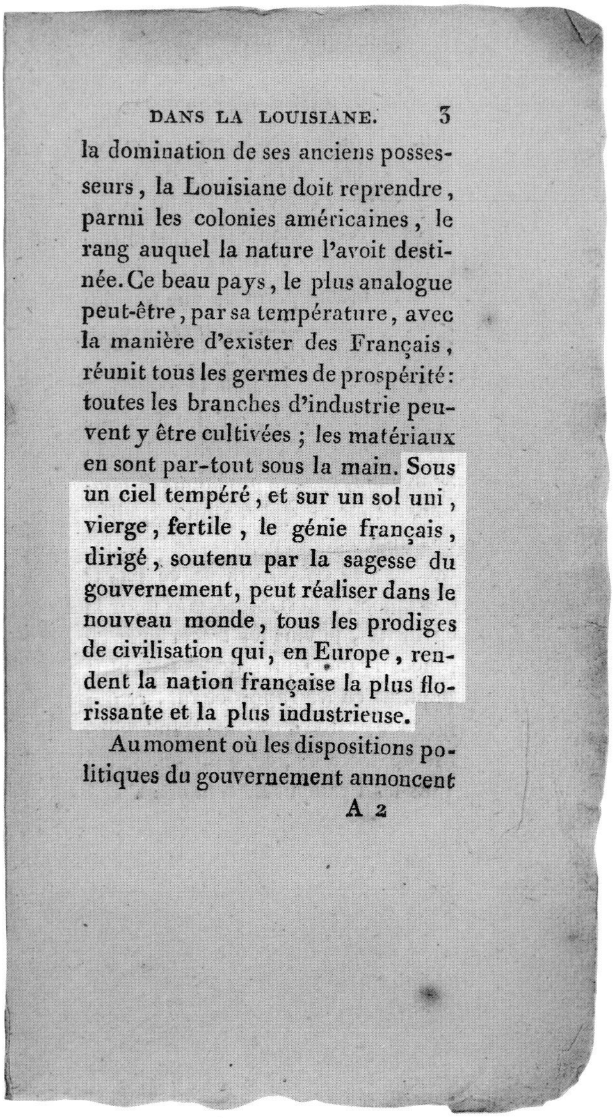

DANS LA LOUISIANE. 3

la domination de ses anciens possesseurs, la Louisiane doit reprendre, parmi les colonies américaines, le rang auquel la nature l'avoit destinée. Ce beau pays, le plus analogue peut-être, par sa température, avec la manière d'exister des Français, réunit tous les germes de prospérité : toutes les branches d'industrie peuvent y être cultivées ; les matériaux en sont par-tout sous la main. Sous un ciel tempéré, et sur un sol uni, vierge, fertile, le génie français, dirigé, soutenu par la sagesse du gouvernement, peut réaliser dans le nouveau monde, tous les prodiges de civilisation qui, en Europe, rendent la nation française la plus florissante et la plus industrieuse.

Au moment où les dispositions politiques du gouvernement annoncent

A 2

Fig. VII.2 Page from Dubroca, *L'itinéraire des Français dans la Louisiane* (1802).
One of the numerous appeals in 1802–03 for French emigrants to Louisiana, recently recovered from Spain. The virgin soil of this land so similar to France in climate, in combination with the genius of Frenchmen guided by the state, would certainly allow the development of a civilization not inferior to that of *la belle France*.

nation of a decade of such pressure. The Girondins, a political group enthusiastic about the spread of the Revolution, had evinced strong interest in Louisiana in 1792. But probably it was the famous Talleyrand who planted the seed in Napoleon's mind. An exile to England and then to the United States in the middle 1790s, Talleyrand developed friendships with such notable émigrés as Malouet and Moreau de Saint-Méry, with whom he discussed relocation (from Philadelphia) to Louisiana. He had high hopes for the territory as a counter to the United States. In any case, Napoleon entered into tough and long bargaining with the Spaniards before he could bribe them to part with Louisiana. He could not persuade them, however, to give up West Florida (ceded to Spain by Britain at the Treaty of Paris, 1783).

In 1802, Napoleon prepared an expedition for the occupation of what was now French Louisiana. In that year and the next, a barrage of books on Louisiana was published to whet French appetites, including Louis Dubroca's *L'itinéraire des Français dans la Louisiane* (Paris, 1802) [132] and Nicholas Jacquemin's *Mémoire sur la Louisiane* (Paris, 1803) [133].

In Saint Domingue, meanwhile, General Leclerc, brother-in-law of Napoleon, led a strong force of twenty thousand troops to overawe Toussaint and return the colony to French rule. Arriving in early 1802 his initial successes were numerous: surrender of the black generals and the retirement of Toussaint to his estate; the allegiance of the remaining whites and most mulattoes despite Toussaint's favorable treatment of them; the later arrest of Toussaint and his embarkation to France where he died in prison; and a crackdown on "Bostonian" traders. Leclerc could thank his army for these triumphs but also the disenchantment of freedmen with Toussaint's forced labor policies and with his favoritism to whites.

Soon, however, Leclerc's triumphs turned sour. Many of his men, just like the British before them, became sick and died of yellow fever. Rumors about the reestablishment of slavery at Guadeloupe increased the unease of freedmen. Some prominent black military leaders, such as Jean-Jacques Dessalines, joined the small liberation movements in the mountains. Leclerc himself died of yellow fever in November 1802, to be replaced by Rochambeau. For one year the son of the old hero of the American Revolution struggled against the resurgent black forces, tropical disease, and then with the renewal of Franco-British hostilities, a suffocating blockade. He surrendered to the British in 1803 and thus the pearl of the Antilles slipped from France's imperial necklace.

On hearing the news of Leclerc's death and the disastrous situation at Saint Domingue, Napoleon reportedly muttered, "Damn sugar, damn coffee, damn colonies." These ill winds from the Caribbean and the renewed prospects for war with Britain influenced Napoleon in his impetuous decision to sell Louisiana to the United States. It is true that Napoleon never ceased to think of colonial empires and often had an open ear for Malouet's schemes, but the primacy of his dreams for European conquest meant war with Britain. A colonial empire was incompatible with continental hegemony.

With the abandonment of Saint Domingue and the sale of Louisiana, little remained of the proud French empire in America. At the Treaty of Vienna in 1815, France retained only Guadeloupe, Martinique and their dependencies, St. Pierre and Miquelon in the north Atlantic for the "dry" fisheries, and Guiana in South America. But the exploits of Champlain and d'Esnambuc, the evangelical labors of Fathers Le Jeune and Breton, and the political skills of Tracy and Bienville were not in vain. Millions of French-speaking peoples of the Americas remain a testimony to that epoch of empire.

INDEX TO AUTHORS AND TITLES OF PRIMARY SOURCES CITED IN THE CATALOGUE*

*Numbers in brackets refer to the numbered List of Primary Sources in the frontmatter. The order of the list of these sources is roughly the order of mention of these works in the text.

Breton, Raymond. *Dictionaire caraibe-françois* (1665) **[64]**

Brief discours des choses plus remarquables (1602) [25]

Briève relation du voyage des isles de l'Amérique (1646) **[51]**

Brissot de Warville, Jacques-Pierre. *Mémoire sur les noirs de l'Amérique septentrionale* (1789) **[118]**

Broë, S. de, translator. See: Solís, Antonio de. *Histoire de la conquête du Mexique.*

Carli, Giovanni Rinaldo. *Lettres américaines* (1788) **[128]**

Cartier, Jacques. *Discours du voyage* (1598) [7]

Casas, Bartolomé de las. *Tyrannies et cruautéz des Espagnols* (1630) **[14]**

Cauxois, Robert Regnauld, translator. See: Acosta, José de. *Histoire naturelle et morale des Indes.*

Champigny, Jean Bochart, chevalier de. *La Louisiane ensanglantée* (1773) **[122]**

Champlain, Samuel de. *Brief discours des choses plus remarquables* (1602) **[25]**

Champlain, Samuel de. *Des sauvages, ou, voyage* (1603) **[26]**

Champlain, Samuel de. *Les voyages de la Nouvelle France occidentale, dicte Canada* (1632) **[34]**

Chanvalon, Jean Baptiste Mathieu Thibault de. *Voyage à la Martinique* (1763) **[104]**

Charlevoix, Pierre-François-Xavier de. *Histoire de l'isle espagnole ou de S. Domingue* (1730–1731) **[90]**

Charlevoix, Pierre-François-Xavier de. *Histoire et description générale de la Nouvelle France* (1744) **[76]**

Chastellux, François Jean. *Voyage de Mr. le chevalier de Chastellux en Amérique* (1785) **[126]**

Chauveton, Urbain, translator. See: Benzoni, Girolamo. *Histoire nouvelle du Nouveau Monde.*

Claude, d'Abbeville. *Histoire de la mission des pères capucins* (1614) **[30]**

Clodoré, Jean. *Relation de ce qui s'est passé dans les isles & terre-ferme de l'Amérique* (1671) **[60]**

Compagnie de la France équinoxiale. *Mémoire pour servir de brève instruction* (1653) **[46]**

Condorcet, Marie Jean Antoine Nicolas Caritat, marquis de. *Réflexions sur l'esclavage des nègres* (1781) **[114]**

Considérations sur l'état présent de la colonie française de Saint-Domingue (1776–1777) **[111]**

Coppie d'une lettre venant de la Floride envoyée à Rouen (1565) **[10]**

Cortés, Hernán. *Des marches, îles et pays trouvés* (1522) **[1]**

La cosmographie. Apian (1544) **[5]**

La cosmographie universelle. Münster (1568) **[6]**

La cosmographie universelle. Thevet (1575) **[18]**

La cosmographie universelle de tout le monde Münster (1575) **[20]**

Coulon, Jean Philippe Garran de. See: Garran de Coulon, Jean Philippe.

Cugnet, François Joseph. *Traité de la police* (1775) **[123]**

Dablon, Claude. *Relation de ce qui s'est passé de plus remarquable* (1672) **[68]**

Dernières découvertes dans l'Amérique septentrionale (1697) **[75]**

Des marches, îles et pays trouvés (1522) **[1]**

Des sauvages, ou, voyage (1603) **[26]**

La descente faite par les François en la terre ferme de l'Amérique (1653) **[47]**

Description de la France équinoctiale (1666) **[59]**

Description de la Louisiane (1683) **[72]**

Description des plantes de l'Amérique (1693) **[87]**

Description géographique de la Guiane (1763) **[107]**

Description topographique et politique de la partie espagnole de l'isle Saint-Domingue (1796) **[119]**

Dictionaire caraibe-françois (1665) **[64]**

Dictionnaire galibi (1763) **[108]**

Discours de l'histoire de la Florida (1566) **[16]**

Le Jeune, Paul. *Relation de ce qui s'est passé en la Nouvelle France, es années 1640 et 1641* (1642) [**38**]

Le Page du Pratz. *Histoire de Louisiane* (1758) [**96**]

Léry, Jean de. *Histoire d'un voyage fait en la terre du Brésil* (1578) [**21**]

Lescarbot, Marc. *Histoire de la Nouvelle France* (1609) [**27**]

L'Etang, Simon Philibert de La Salle de. See: La Salle de l'Etang, Simon Philibert de.

Lettres américaines (1788) [**128**]

Lettres patentes (1717) [**93**]

Lettres-patentes (1763) [**106**]

Loix et constitutions des colonies françoises (1784–1790) [**39**]

López de Gómara, Francisco. *Histoire géneralle des Indes Occidentales* (1605) [**11**]

La Louisiane ensanglantée (1773) [**122**]

Maison rustique (1763) [**105**]

Malouet, Pierre-Victor. *Mémoire sur l'esclavage des nègres* (1788) [**113**]

Martyr, Peter. See: Anghiera, Pietro Martire d'.

Maurile de Saint Michel. *Voyage des isles Camercanes* (1652) [**52**]

Mazzei, Filippo. *Recherches historiques et politiques sur les Etats-Unis de l'Amérique septentrionale* (1788) [**127**]

M.D.L.S. *Dictionnaire galibi* (1763) [**108**]

Mémoire en faveur des gens de couleur (1789) [**129**]

Mémoire pour servir de brève instruction (1653) [**46**]

Mémoire sur la Louisiane (1803) [**133**]

Mémoire sur l'esclavage des nègres (1788) [**113**]

Mémoire sur les causes des troubles et des désastres de la colonie de Saint-Domingue (1793) [**130**]

Mémoire sur les noirs de l'Amérique septentrionale (1789) [**118**]

Mémoires historiques sur la Louisiane (1753) [**97**]

Mémoires pour servir à l'histoire de Cayenne (1777) [**109**]

Merveilles, Blaise François de Pagan, comte de. See: Pagan, Blaise François de, comte de.

Miggrode, Jacques de, translator. See: Casas, Bartolomé de las. *Tyrannies et cruautez des Espagnols.*

Le miroir du monde (1579) [**13**]

Mocquet, Jean. *Voyages en Afrique, Asie, Indes Orientales, & Occidentales* (1645) [**28**]

Moeurs des sauvages amériquains (1724) [**99**]

Monsieur N***, supposed author. See: *Voyages aux côtes de Guinée & en Amérique.*

Montaboddo, Fracanzano da. See: Fracanzano da Montaboddo.

Montigny, Dumont de. See: Dumont de Montigny.

Moreau de Saint-Méry, Médéric Louis Elie. *Description topographique et politique de la partie espagnole de l'isle Saint-Domingue* (1796) [**119**]

Moreau de Saint-Méry, Médéric Louis Elie, editor. See: France. *Loix et constitutions des colonies françoises.*

Münster, Sebastian. *La cosmographie universelle* (1568) [**6**]

Münster, Sebastian. *La cosmographie universelle de tout le monde* (1575) [**20**]

Le Nouveau Monde et navigacions faites par Emeric de Vespuce (1516) [**3**]

Nouveau voyage aux isles de l'Amérique (1722) [**63**]

Nouveau voyage dans l'Amérique septentrionale (1782) [**125**]

Nouveau voyage d'un pais plus grand que l'Europe (1698) [**74**]

Nouveaux voyages. Lahontan (1703) [**71**]

Nouveaux voyages aux Indes Occidentales (1768) [**98**]

Nouveaux voyages dans l'Amérique septentrionale (1777) [**121**]

Nouvelle découverte de plusieurs nations dans la Nouvelle France en l'année 1673 et 1674 (n.d.) [**69**]

Nouvelle relation. Gage (1676) [**66**]

Nouvelle relation de la France équinoxiale (1743) [**89**]

Nouvelles considérations sur Saint-Domingue (1780) [**115**]

Oexmelin, Alexandre Olivier. See: Exquemelin, Alexandre Olivier.

Ortelius, Abraham. *Théâtre de l'univers* (1598) [**12**]

Oviedo y Valdés, Gonzalo Fernández de. See: Fernández de Oviedo y Valdés, Gonzalo.

Pacifique, de Provins. *Briève relation du voyage des isles de l'Amérique* (1646) [**51**]

Pagan, Blaise François de, comte de Merveilles. *Relation historique et géographique* (1655) [**50**]

Pelleprat, Pierre. *Relation des missions des PP. de la Compagnie de Jésus* (1655) [**43**]

Peter Martyr. See: Anghiera, Pietro Martire d'.

Pigafetta, Antonio. *Le voyage et navigation* (1525) [**8**]

Plumier, Charles. *Description des plantes de l'Amérique* (1693) [**87**]

Pointis, Jean-Bernard-Louis Desjean, baron de. *Relation de l'expédition de Carthagène* (1698) [**79**]

Préfontaine, chevalier de. *Maison rustique* (1763) [**105**]

Proiet d'une compagnie pour l'Amérique (1651) [**45**]

Provins, Pacifique de. See: Pacifique, de Provins.

Pyrard, François. *Voyage* (1619) [**29**]

Ragueneau, Paul. *Relation de ce qui s'est passé de plus remarquable* (1652) [**55**]

Raimond, Julien. *Mémoire sur les causes des troubles et des désastres de la colonie de Saint-Domingue* (1793) [**130**]

Rapport sur les troubles de Saint-Domingue (1797–1799) [**131**]

Raymond, Julien. See: Raimond, Julien.

Raynal, abbé. *Essai sur l'administration de St. Domingue* (1785) [**116**]

Raynal, abbé. *Histoire philosophique et politique des établissemens et du commerce des Européens dans les deux Indes* (1780) [**117**]

Recherches historiques et politiques sur les Etats-Unis de l'Amérique septentrionale (1788) [**127**]

Recueil de divers voyages faits en Afrique et en l'Amérique (1674) [**61**]

Recueil de voyages. Thévenot (1681) [**70**]

Recueil de voyages au Nord (1725–1738) [**95**]

Redouer, Mathurin du, translator. See: *Le Nouveau Monde et navigacions faites par Emeric de Vespuce.*

Réflexions sur l'esclavage des nègres (1781) [**114**]

Regnauld Cauxois, Robert. See: Cauxois, Robert Regnauld.

Relation abrégée d'un voyage (1745) [**88**]

Relation de ce qui s'est passé cette année en Canada (1755) [**102**]

Relation de ce qui s'est passé dans les isles & terre-ferme de l'Amérique (1671) [**60**]

Relation de ce qui s'est passé de plus remarquable. Ragueneau (1652) [**55**]

Relation de ce qui s'est passé de plus remarquable. Lallemant (1661) [**56**]

Relation de ce qui s'est passé de plus remarquable. Le Jeune (1662) [**57**]

Relation de ce qui s'est passé de plus remarquable. Dablon (1672) [**68**]

Relation de ce qui s'est passé en Canada (1691) [**83**]

Relation de ce qui s'est passé en la Nouvelle France en l'année 1633. Le Jeune (1634) [**37**]

Relation de ce qui s'est passé en la Nouvelle France en l'année 1642 & 1643. Vimont (1644) [**54**]

Relation de ce qui s'est passé en la Nouvelle France, es années 1640 et 1641. Le Jeune (1642) [**38**]

Relation de la Nouvelle France (1616) [**32**]

Relation de la rivière des Amazones (1682) [**62**]

Relation de l'éstablissement des François depuis l'an 1635 (1640) [**42**]

Relation de l'expédition de Carthagène (1698) [**79**]

Relation des missions des PP. de la Compagnie de Jésus (1655) [**43**]

Relation du voyage des François fait au Cap de Nord en Amérique (1654) [**48**]

Relation d'un voyage de la Mer du Sud (1715) [**78**]

SELECTED SECONDARY SOURCES

It is clearly unjust to single out as being particularly important a mere handful of the hundreds of important books and articles related to the themes of this catalogue. The works cited below, however, were indispensable to the author in the preparation of this book.

Adair, E.R. "France and the Beginnings of New France." *Canadian Historical Review* 25 (1944):246–278.

Atkinson, Geoffrey. *Les nouveaux horizons de la Renaissance française.* Paris, 1935.

Biggar, H.P. *Early Trading Companies of New France.* Toronto, 1901.

Boiteux, L.A. *Richelieu: Grand Maître de la navigation et du commerce de France.* Paris, 1955.

Braudel, F., *et al.*, eds. *Le Monde de Jacques Cartier.* Montreal, 1984.

Chaunu, Pierre. "La légende noire anti-hispanique." *Revue historique* 229 (1963): 59–102.

Chinard, Gilbert. *L'Amérique et le rêve exotique dans la littérature française aux xviie et xviiie siècles.* Paris, 1912.

Cole, Charles W. *Colbert and a Century of French Mercantilism.* New York, 1939.

Cultru, Prosper. "La colonisation d'autrefois: le Commandeur de Poincy à St. Christophe." *Revue de l'histoire des colonies françaises* 3 (1915):289–354.

Dainville, François. *La géographie des humanistes.* Paris, 1940.

Dampierre, Jacques. *Essai sur les sources de l'histoire des Antilles françaises, 1492–1664.* Paris, 1904.

Debien, Gabriel. "Les engagés pour les Antilles." *Revue de l'histoire des colonies* 38 (1951):1–280.

Delumeau, Jean. "Le commerce extérieur français au xviie siècle." *Dix-septième siècle* 70–71 (1966):80–105.

Devèze, Michel. *Antilles, Guyanes, la mer des Caraibes.* Paris, 1977.

De Vorsey, Louis. "La Salle's Cartography of the Lower Mississippi: Product of Error or Deception?" *Geoscience and Man* 25 (1988):5–23.

Dickason, Olive. *The Myth of the Savage and Early French Colonialism in the Americas.* Edmonton, Alberta, 1983.

Eccles, W.J. *The Canadian Frontier.* New York, 1969.

_____. *France in America.* New York, 1972.

Frostin, C. *Les révoltes blanches à Saint Domingue aux xviie et xviiie siècles.* Paris, 1975.

Galloway, Pat, ed. *La Salle and His Legacy.* Jackson, Mississippi 1982.

Geggus, David. *Slavery, War and Revolution: The British Occupation of Saint Domingue.* Oxford, 1982.

Giraud, Marcel. *Histoire de la Louisiane française.* 4 vols. Paris, 1953–74.

Hauser, H. *La pensée et l'action économique du Cardinal de Richelieu.* Paris, 1944.

Heulhard, A. *Villegaignon: Roi d'Amérique.* Paris, 1897.

Hogden, Margaret. *Early Anthropology in the Sixteenth and Seventeenth Centuries.* Philadelphia, 1964.

Hurault, Jean. *Français et Indiens en Guyane: 1604–1972.* Paris, 1972.

Jaenen, Cornelius. *Friend and Foe: Aspects of French-Amerindian Cultural Contact in the Sixteenth and Seventeenth Centuries.* New York, 1976.

———. *The Role of the Church in New France.* Toronto, 1976.

Julien, Charles-André. *Les voyages de découverte et les premiers établissements, xve, xvie siècles.* Paris, 1948.

Lamontagne, Roland. "L'influence de Colbert sur l'oeuvre de Jean Talon." *Revue d'histoire de l'Amérique française* 4 (1952):42–61.

La Roncière, Ch. de. *Histoire de la marine française.* 6 vols. Paris, 1909–32.

Lokke, Carl. *France and the Colonial Question.* New York, 1968.

Lyon, E. Wilson. *Louisiana in French Diplomacy, 1759–1804.* Norman, Oklahoma., 1934.

Lyon, Eugene. *The Enterprise of Florida: Pedro Menéndez de Avilés and the Spanish Conquest of 1565–1568.* Gainesville, Florida 1976.

Meyer, Jean. "La France et les puissances maritimes." *Dix-septième siècle* 123 (1979): 155–172.

Mims, Stewart. *Colbert's West India Policy.* New Haven, 1912.

Rennard, Joseph. *Baas, Blénac: ou, les Antilles françaises du xviie siècle.* Fort-de-France, Martinique, 1935.

———. *Histoire religieuse des Antilles françaises des origines à 1914.* Paris, 1954.

Saintoyant, J. *La colonisation française sous l'ancien régime.* 2 vols. Paris, 1929.

———. *La colonisation française pendant la Révolution, 1789–99.* 2 vols. Paris, 1930.

See, Henri. "Que faut-il penser de l'oeuvre économique de Colbert?" *Revue historique* 152 (1926):98–194.

Servant, Georges. "Les compagnies de St. Christophe et des îles de l'Amérique, 1626–1653." *Revue de l'histoire des colonies françaises* 1 (1913):385–482.

Singh, R. John. *French Diplomacy in the Caribbean and the American Revolution.* Hicksville, New York, 1977.

Tarrade, Jean. *Le commerce colonial de la France à la fin de l'ancien régime.* 2 vols. Paris, 1972.

Trudel, Marcel. *Histoire de la Nouvelle France: vol. III: La Seigneurie des Cents-Associés, 1627–1663.* Tome 1: Les événements. Montreal, 1979.

Vaumas, Guillaume. *L'éveil missionnaire de la France.* Lyons, 1942.

Wood, Peter. "La Salle: Discovery of a Lost Explorer." *American Historical Review* 89 (1982):294–323.

Wroth, L. C. *Acts of the French Royal Administration Concerning Canada, Guiana, the West Indies and Louisiana prior to 1791.* New York, 1930.

Readers interested in probing further the history of overseas France should consult, among others, the *Revue de l'histoire des colonies* (later, *Revue française d'histoire d'outremer*), the *Revue de l'histoire de l'Amérique française,* and the *Proceedings of the French Colonial Historical Society,* vols. 1–12.

SUGGESTIONS FOR FURTHER READING

The works listed below will provide for the English-language reader further information on some of the topics treated in this catalogue.

Alvord, Clarence. *The Illinois Country, 1673–1818*. Chicago, 1965.

Axtell, James. *The Invasion Within: The Contest of Cultures in Colonial North America*. New York, 1985.

Brebner, J.B. *The Explorers of North America, 1492–1806*. London, 1933.

Crouse, Nellis. *French Pioneers in the West Indies, 1624–1664*. New York, 1940.

_____. *The French Struggle for the West Indies, 1665–1713*. New York, 1948.

_____. *Le Moyne d'Iberville: Soldier of New France*. Ithaca, New York, 1954.

Dull, Jonathan. *The French Navy and American Independence*. Princeton, 1975.

Eccles, W.J. *Frontenac: the Courtier Governor*. Toronto, 1959.

_____. *Canada under Louis XIV, 1663–1701*. Toronto, 1964.

Ekberg, Carl. *Colonial Ste. Genevieve*. St. Louis, 1985.

Giraud, Marcel. *A History of French Louisiana, Vol. I: The Reign of Louis XIV, 1698–1715*. Baton Rouge, 1974.

Higginbotham, Jay. *Old Mobile: Fort Louis de la Louisiane, 1702–1711*. Mobile, 1977.

Jaenen, Cornelius. *The French Relationship with the Native Peoples of New France and Acadia*. Ottawa, 1984.

James, C.L.R. *The Black Jacobins*. New York, 1963.

Lanctot, Gustave. *A History of Canada*. 3 vols. Cambridge, Massachusetts, 1963–65.

Murphy, Edmund. *Henry de Tonty: Fur Trader of the Mississippi*. Baltimore, 1941.

Ott, Thomas. *The Haitian Revolution*. Knoxville, Tennessee, 1973.

Parkman, Frances. *Montcalm and Wolfe*. Boston, 1844.

_____. *A Half Century of Conflict*. Boston, 1892.

_____. *La Salle and the Discovery of the Great West*. Boston, 1908.

Priestley, Herbert I. *France Overseas throughout the Old Regime*. New York, 1939.

Reinhardt, Steven, ed. *The Sun King: Louis XIV and the New World*. New Orleans, 1984.

Roberts, W.A. *The French in the West Indies*. New York, 1971.

Trudel, Marcel. *The Beginnings of New France, 1524–1663*. Toronto, 1973.

Woods, Patricia D. *French-Indian Relations on the Southern Frontier, 1699–1762*. Ann Arbor, Michigan, 1980.

Zoltvany, Yves F. *The French Tradition in America*. New York, 1969.

INDEX

LES NOUVELLES FRANCES
France in America, 1500–1815
An Imperial Perspective

This book was designed by Gilbert Associates
and printed by Reynolds-DeWalt Printing
on Bowaters Gleneagle paper.

The type is Fournier, cut for Monotype
in 1924. The design is named after, and based on
the work of, the eighteenth-century
French designer Pierre-Simon Fournier.

The book was bound by Mueller Trade Binders.

1,200 copies for the John Carter Brown Library.

April 1989